HARRY HILL'S

WHOPPING GREAT JOKE BOOK

faber and faber

For Archer/Quinnell
– one of the great double acts

First published in 2008
This edition first published 2017
by Faber and Faber Limited
Bloomsbury House, 74–77 Great Russell Street,
London WC1B 3DA

Printed and bound by CPI Group (UK) Ltd, Croydon, CR0 4YY
Design by Faber and Faber Ltd

A CIP record for this book
is available from the British Library

ISBN 978-0-571-34120-7

FSC
www.fsc.org
MIX
Paper from
responsible sources
FSC® C101712

2 4 6 8 10 9 7 5 3

H. HILL

BESPOKE JOKES TO THE GENTRY

BY APPOINTMENT TO HER MAJESTY THE PEARLY QUEEN ELIZABETH OF HACKNEY

ALSO I ONCE MET THE CHUCKLE BROTHERS

HILL TOWERS

LONDON

Dear Fellow Comedian,

Never underestimate the power of jokes! If you can make someone laugh you can control them, albeit for only a few moments. What you hold in your hands is a very valuable thing: nothing less than a mind-control handbook!

I have scoured the great Joke archives in all the libraries of the world from Maidstone (in Kent) to Timbuktu (in East Sussex); indeed I went even further – to Timbukthree (Hampshire/Surrey borders) – and have chosen only the funny ones. On top of that I've given you some of my own jokes which I have told every night for twenty years and have always got a laugh with (except at the Norwegian Comedy Festival; I blame the audience). If that were not enough, I and an associate (Mr Peter Quinnell of Hastings) have even written some new ones. Basically, if you can't raise a laugh out of this little book then you've had it and, in the words of Simon Cowell, 'You're not coming to London.'

Oh yes, with this book and the mind-bending power held therein you could take over little short of the world. But a word of warning. Use that power only for good. If you use it wrongly your hair will fall out.

Enjoy the book – it's a great life!

Your Friend in Laughter,

Harry Hill

Harry Hill

PS: If I've missed any out please send them in to Faber and Faber, Bloomsbury House, 74–77 Great Russell Street, London, WC1B 3DA. And together we'll write Book 2.

HOW TO TELL A JOKE

1. Work up a routine of about five minutes of your favourite jokes. Work out which ones go best and open your routine with your best joke and finish it with your second best joke.

2. Get a good outfit. Then when you've got a good outfit – move around a bit and show 'em the outfit. That way your audience will think you're a success even if you aren't, yet.

3. Shakespeare once said that brevity is the soul of wit – don't worry, I don't know what he was on about either. My advice is you won't get many laughs spouting Shakespeare – stick to jokes.

4. Make sure that if there's a light on in the room you're standing under it. Ideally you should be the focus of attention — that's why comedy seldom works in a restaurant.

5. Make sure they can hear you. If they can't hear you it's like watching fish. When did a fish last make you laugh? Exactly.

6. Wait for the laugh. But not too long. As a rule, if there's a change of season whilst you're waiting it's probably time to move on to the next one.

7. If it's going badly — get off.

8. If it's going well — get off. Don't outstay your welcome.

9. Keep all receipts. The reason for this will become clear to you when you're a bit older and have to start paying a thing called Tax. (See Ken Dodd.)

10. Don't blame the audience — except at the Norwegian Comedy Festival.

11. Go and see comedians working live or watch them on DVDs and study how they do it. Particularly me. Ask your parents to buy you my DVDs and tickets to my shows. Do that now. Keep pestering them until they do it.

12. Keep going. That's it, just keep going – it's all you can do.

13. Have fun. This is the most important one. Never let it seem like work – this life you've chosen for yourself of telling jokes. It ain't work. Sitting in an office watching other people having fun – that's work. You and me? We're the ones who escaped.

THE JOKES

ACCIDENTS

POLICEMAN: Did you get the number of the woman who knocked you over?
PEDESTRIAN: No, but I'd recognise that laugh anywhere.

I broke my leg in two places – Sheffield and Wolverhampton.

AGEING

I come from a family of long livers. My dad had a liver three feet long.

liver

Gall bladder (size of a crisp packet)
(Ready salted)

Will you love me when I'm old and wrinkled?
Of course I do.

Did you hear about the blind grandfather who went sky-diving?
He had a great time, but his guide dog was terrified.

ALIENS

Which green plastic flaky substance is found on aliens' scalps?
Astroscurf.

You know when people say they've been abducted by aliens – they always describe them as having a big head, big black eyes. I wonder if they've really been abducted by pandas instead and are just too embarrassed to say!

How does a Martian know when he's attractive?
When bits of metal stick to him.

If a flying saucer is an aircraft, does that make a flying broomstick a witchcraft?

What did the alien say to the petrol pump?
'Take your finger out of your nose when I am talking to you!'

What sort of sweets do
Martians eat?
Martian mallows.

How do you know when an
alien has been in your
fridge?
There's a note saying
'Sorry I used all the milk,
signed An Alien.'

Why do aliens have such
terrible trouble drinking tea?
Flying saucers.

RUMBLE
RUMBLE

What did the hungry alien say when it landed on Earth?
Take me to your larder.

Did you hear about the man who was kidnapped by teddy bears from outer space?
He had a close encounter of the furred kind.

What should you do if you find a green alien?
Wait until it is ripe.

There was a big football match on the planet
Mars and one of the Martian players tripped his
opponent in the penalty area.
'Right,' said the referee, 'I'm booking you
for that. What's your name?'
'XXXYYLXMXXXLLLMXXXXXXYXXXXKKKKKXX-
KKVVGGGHHHKKXXKKAAAKKGGGGXXCCC-
KKKKKKKKKX.'
'On second thoughts, I'll let you off with
a warning.'

Which horse-drawn cart did the aliens use to
deliver their beer?
The Dray of the Triffids.

What do you call a sad spaceship?
An unidentified crying object.

ANIMALS

What can you use to smooth out walruses?
Seal Irons.

Mm that's hot... but nice!

What is brown and fizzy and lives in eucalyptus trees?
Coca-Koala.

What is brown and fizzy, lives in eucalyptus trees
and has lost weight recently?
Diet Coca-Koala.

What is brown and fizzy, lives in eucalyptus trees
and has been run over by a steam roller?
Flat Coca-Koala.

I took my guinea pig to
Cheddar Gorge.
Cavy?
That's an understatement!

CHEDDAR GORGE

I can't
smell any
cheese!

Why was the mummy glow-worm unhappy?
Because her children weren't very bright.

What animal goes 'Oooo'?
A cow with no lips.

<Pardon?

What animal does a Canadian have for pudding?
A moose.

What's green and hangs in a tree?
Giraffe snot.

Why don't pigs eat bacon?
They can't operate the grill.

What do you call a monkey with one leg?
A wonky.

What do you call a donkey with three legs?
A wonky donkey.

What's pink and goes 'Moo'?
A pig with an identity crisis.

What do you call a one-legged monkey on the
back of a three-legged donkey?
A cry for help.

What do baby apes sleep in?
Apri-cots.

What's brown, prickly and squirts red stuff?
A hedgehog eating a doughnut.

What's brown, prickly and squirts white stuff?
A hedgehog eating a cream puff.

What's brown, prickly and squirts green stuff?
A hedgehog with a chest infection. (Yuk!)

REARGH!

What did the skunk say when the wind changed direction?
It's all coming back to me now!

What goes, 'Now you see me, now you don't; now you see me, now you don't'?
A penguin on a zebra crossing.

What do you get if you pour hot water down a rabbit hole?
A hot cross bunny.

I'm not coming round to YOU at Easter!

What's orange and sounds like a parrot?
A carrot!

What's orange and sounds like a hedgehog?
An hedgehog pretending to be a goldfish.

Why did the squirrels bury the acorns?
It's just what the oak tree wants –
they're playing right into his hands.

ARGUMENTS

Look, I'll meet you half-way: I'll admit you're
wrong if you'll admit I'm right.

I won't say she's argumentative, but even her
waxwork answers back.

ART

How do you go about carving a statue of an angel?
It's easy. You just get a block of marble and chip away everything that doesn't look like an angel.

I bought a painting from a junk shop. When I got it home, I took it to the Antiques Roadshow and asked the expert what he thought of it.
He said, 'The good news is it's a genuine De la Wantini, over a hundred years old. The bad news is that De La Wantini was a plumber.'

AUSTRALIA

What do you call a boomerang that doesn't come back?
A stick.

I'm not going anywhere...
I like it here.

I'm still searching

How do you surprise an Australian pudding?
Boo! Meringue!

What's red and green and hops round the outback?
Kanga-rhubarb.

G'Day!
No worries! Howzat!
and other Australian phrases.

BABIES

But, darling, this isn't our baby!
I know, but it's a much nicer pram!

What's the new baby's name?
I don't know. We can't understand a word
he says!

BLURBLE!

Funny name for a Baby!

PROUD FATHER: My new baby looks just like me!
NURSE: Well, never mind. As long as it's healthy.

When he was born he was so ugly that the doctor slapped his mother.

How come you were born in Edinburgh?
I wanted to be near my mother.

BALDNESS

The only way I know to keep your hair from falling out is to knot it from the inside.

They're marketing a new cure for baldness. It doesn't grow hair, it just shrinks your head to fit what hair you've got left.

BARBER: How was that lotion I gave you for growing hair on your bald patch?
CUSTOMER: Well, my head's still bald but I have to shave my fingers twice a day!

What is a complete waste of time?
Telling a hair-raising story to a bald man.

BALLOONS

What do you call an adult balloon?
A blown-up.

What's the quickest way to blow up a balloon?
Dynamite.

BATHROOM

How did the bubbles communicate?
By mobile foam.

Two monkeys were getting in a bath. One said,
'Oo, oo, oo, aah, aah, aah.'
The other monkey said, 'Well put some cold
in, then.'

What should you do if lightning strikes your
lavatory?
Don't panic – it's just a flash in the pan.

Why did Tigger look down the toilet?
To find Pooh.

I collected the dirty froth off the bathtub and
sent it to London to be analysed.
Post scum? (Post's come.)
Oh good – is that a letter from the lab?

I think my bathroom is haunted. I keep hearing
weird knocking noises and the sink doesn't seem
to fill up properly.
Strange taps?
Exactly!

Why did the toilet paper roll down the hill?
Because it wanted to get to the bottom.

BEAUTY

Why did the girl have a pile of dirt on her shoulder?
Because she had a mole on her cheek.

She's had her face lifted so many times, it's out of focus.

I have five eyes, six ears and three mouths. What am I?
Quite ugly.

Hello. I've come about the nose job!

She spent five hours at the beauty salon – just getting a price.

She wanted to have her face lifted but it proved impossible. So, for half the price, they lowered her body.

She was amazing! That girl had everything a man could want: big muscles, a beard, a moustache . . .

Why can't your nose be twelve inches long?
Because it would be a foot!

Do you ever file your nails?
No, I just cut them off and throw them away!

My brother's got a great head on his shoulders.
Yes, but it would look a lot better on his neck.

BEES

What do bees chew?
Buzzle gum.

Bzzzz

" "

— concentrate
on the job
in hand mate!

MOTHER: Poor Leona, did the bee sting you?
LEONA (*sobbing*): Yes!
MOTHER: Let's put some cream on it then.
LEONA: Don't be silly – it'll be miles away by now.

I keep bees – not for honey – for the fur! The pelt of the bee makes excellent pea cosies, and the flesh of the bee is packed full of vitamins – particularly vitamin B.

BIRDS

A male swan can break a man's arm with a single twist of its neck.
But a female swan can break a man swan's heart with just a glance.

Which ducks do not rust?
Stainless teal.

Why are parrots always clever?
Because they suck seed.

HARRY: Can you name two birds that can't fly?
ALAN: An ostrich and a dead parrot.

Why does a flamingo lift up one leg?
Because if it lifted up both legs it would fall over!

I knew I shouldn't have done that but I was just curious.

BIRTHDAYS

A friend of mine lives in a castle in Scotland. It was his daughter's second birthday. So he put an inflatable council estate in the garden.

Was there anyone famous born on your birthday?
No, only small babies.

What do you say to cows on their birthday?
'Happy birthday to moo.'

I can't blow them out 'cos I haven't got any lips

let me have a go!

How does a mussel celebrate her birthday?
She shell-ebrates!

I found the perfect thing for your birthday . . .
No-thing!

I'd like to buy my mum some lipstick for her
birthday, only I'm not sure what size her mouth is.

Did you hear about the stupid boy who tried to
make his sister a birthday cake?
The candles melted in the oven.

Where would you find a present for your cat's
birthday?
In a cat-alogue.

What's your favourite type of present?
Another one.

We didn't put candles on Granny's birthday cake this year – we wanted to prevent global warming.

ALAN: Birthday cake gives me heartburn.
HARRY: Try blowing out the candles before you eat it.

BISCUITS

Why did the cookie cry?
'Cos her mother had been a wafer so long.

What do the gingerbread school children do on the last day of term?
They break up.

Why did the blind gingerbread men visit the Royal Mint?
Because it makes currants-see.

Why did the cookie go to the hospital?
Because it felt crummy.

BOGEYS

LEON: I've just got hold of ultra rare tickets to the Annual Bogey Fête and you haven't.
LEONA: Snot Fair!
LEON: That's right and I can't wait!

What do you call a greenfly with no arms, legs or wings?
A bogey.

BOOKS

Where do they keep the books that aren't true?
The Lie-brary.

What is the baby fruit tree's favourite story?
'The Three Pears'.
How does it end?
They all lived appley every after.

who's been sleeping in my Bowl?!

My Life With Dracula – by Drew Blood.

ALAN: I swallowed the dictionary!
HARRY: Don't breathe a word to anybody!

What lies behind the Balti wardrobe?
Naania.

Why was *The Lord of the Rings'* author told off at school?
For Tolkien in class.

BOXING

What other sport is there where you only wear shorts and Gloves?

I used to be a boxer. I fought Amir Khan once. In the first round, I really had him worried. He thought he'd killed me.

BOXER: Have I done the other guy any damage yet?
TRAINER: No, but keep swinging – the draught might give him a cold.

A very old, unsuccessful fighter was discussing his next move with his trainer. 'I wanna fight Bob Savage!' he says.

'How about Amir Khan?' says the trainer.

'No, I wanna fight Bob Savage!' says the boxer.

'What about Ricky Hatton?'

'Didn't you hear me? I said I wanna fight Bob Savage!'

'Prince Naseem?'

'No! Bob Savage!'

'Mike Tyson?'

'I said Bob Savage!'

'Barry McGuigan?'

'For the last time, I wanna fight Bob Savage!'

To which the trainer finally replies, 'You fool, you ARE Bob Savage!'

BOYS

A little boy got separated from his father at the funfair. 'What's your father like?' asked the attendant.

'Football and going to the pub,' said the boy.

ALAN: Have you got any holes in your pants?
HARRY: Certainly not!
ALAN: Then how do you get your legs through?

BROTHERS

Why don't you take your little brother to the zoo?
If they want him, they can come and get
him.

LEONA: I've got this ferret for my little brother.
JAMELIA: What a brilliant swap!

Do you like my dress?

'For my birthday, I'd like a dress to match the colour of my eyes,' Rebecca said wistfully. 'Blimey! Where am I going to get a bloodshot dress?' said her brother.

LEONA: My brother can do great bird imitations.
JAMELIA: You mean he can copy their voices?
LEONA: No – he eats worms.

A Brother and sister were looking down a wishing well. They both made a wish, and waited expectantly. Suddenly, the sister lost her footing and fell down the well.

'Amazing,' said the boy. 'It really works!'

My little brother was banned from our local leisure centre for weeing in the swimming pool. I told them lots of little boys wee in the swimming pool.

They said, 'Yes, but not from the high-diving board.'

BROWN

What's brown and sticky?
A stick.

What's sticky and brown?
A sticky stick.

BUTCHERS

HARRY: I brought these bacon rashers back. They're bad.
BUTCHER: That's impossible – the bacon was cured only last week.
HARRY: Then it must have had a relapse.

I feel terrible doc'

What do you call someone who peers through a butcher's window?
A mince spy.

My pork butcher's Midlands warehouse has been attacked by arsonists.
Burning ham?
No, it's just outside Coventry.

CANNIBALS

HIC!

Pardon me, it must have been someone I ate!

What's the definition of a cannibal?
Someone who goes into a restaurant and orders the waiter.

What's a cannibal's favourite game?
Swallow the leader.

What's the cannibal's favourite meal?
Kate and Sidney pie.

CARS

I was driving along with my nan and at every corner we went round she's going, 'Oh we're going too fast, slow down, we're going to crash!' I said, 'For pity's sake Nan – move over, I'll drive!'

Why did the wheel go to sleep?
Because it was tyre-d.

Who won the Duffel Coat Grand Prix?
Jensen Toggle.

I'm just going to the petrol station for a twelve-pack of Polos.
How long will you be?
Just over ten mints.

I think the traffic's getting worse. I was trying to cross the road today and after twenty minutes a policeman came up to me and said, 'There's a zebra crossing just round the corner.'
So I said, 'Well, I hope he's having better luck than I am!'

Sorry I'm late. I got held up by the traffic lights.
D'you mean they were stuck on red?
Oh no. They kept changing colour, but they didn't have one I liked.

POLICEMAN: What gear were you in when the accident occurred?
HARRY: Black trousers, jacket and a big-collared shirt. Why?

What do they rub on those metal fences down the middle of the motorways to keep them shiny?
Barrier cream.

I couldn't keep my eyes off this young couple in front of me on the motorway today. They were snogging passionately for about twenty miles.
So what's unusual about that?
They were in separate cars!

POLICEMAN: Why is one side of your car painted red and the other side blue?
HARRY: I like to hear the witnesses contradict each other.

What's round, sad and lives in the boot of your car?
De-spair tyre.

I'm so alone...

HARRY: I'll teach you to throw stones at my new car!

ALAN: I wish you would. I've thrown about five stones and haven't hit it yet!

How do you make anti-freeze?
Hide her woolly blanket.

ALAN: Dad, I'm afraid the car's got water in the carburettor.

HARRY: Where *is* the car?

ALAN: In the lake.

CATS

Got any cat-sup?
...I mean ketchup.

You know there's a black cat in the dining room?
Don't worry, they're supposed to be lucky.
Well this one certainly is. He's eating your
dinner!

HARRY: How do you get milk from a Persian cat?
ALAN: Take his saucer away.

HARRY: Can you help me? I'm looking for a stray cat with one eye.
ALAN: Wouldn't it help if you used both eyes?

Which pet is sort of spiral shaped?
Helix the cat.

HARRY: Careful with that cat, it's worth £250!
ALAN: Gosh, how can a cat save so much money?

CELEBRITY

A simple way to remember the stars' names is to think of sweets:

Cadbury's Cream Egg – Mystic Meg
Curly Wurly – Liz Hurley
Wagon Wheel – Seal
Sherbet Dib Dab – Andy McNab
Candy floss – Jonathan Ross
Milky Bar – Jimmy Carr

Can you think of any others?

Which celebrity made Moses weep?
Jordan.

What was Bruce Lee's favourite dinner?
Karate chops.

I went for an Indian with a supermodel, but the lentils tasted of washing-up liquid.
Soapy Dahl?
No, it was Naomi Campbell.

How did Scary Spice demand attention from her pet seabird?
If you want to be my Plover, you must be my friend!

Which detergent powder did the Beach Boys use to wash their Hawaiian shirts?
Surf.

Which film star is always jumping around the forest?
John Treevaulter.

Which boy band is made of flour, butter, eggs and sugar?
Cake that.

What's pink with yellow spots and big eyes and sings, 'I'm lovin' angels instead'?
Mr Blobby Williams.

I will not be joining Cake That for the ← reunion!

Help! Come quickly! Jordan's just fallen over on the ice and she's only wearing a negligee.
Nasty slip?
I'm afraid so.

HARRY: I recently had a salad on the beach with that singer who had a hit with 'I Wish I Was a Punk Rocker with Flowers in My Hair'.
ALAN: Sandy Thom?
HARRY: Yes, and the cucumber was all gritty.

Did you know that if Amy Winehouse was bitten by a werewolf and then married the chairman of Reading football team – John Madjeski – she would then become Amy Majestic Wine Ware House.

Which Disney favourites are helpful when attempting (unsuccessfully) to repair your leaking camping mattress?
Lilo and Stitch.

Which attractively shy film star has been awarded a bursary to study adhesives?
Glue Grant.

HARRY: I recently asked a soft rock combo who had hits with 'Everything Changes' and 'Somewhere Only We Know' whether they'd like an ice lolly each.
ALAN: Keane?
HARRY: I'll say! I've never seen the ice-cream man pull so many 99s.

HARRY: What do you call a kebab that froths at the mouth and sings 'I'm hung up on you'?
ALAN: A Mad-Donna.

What's green, sits in a salad and sings 'Are you
lonesome tonight?'
Elvis Parsley.

How often does Keira practise acting?
Nightly.

HARRY: I recently went to see an open-air
performance of *Romeo and Juliet* in the winter
and sitting in front of me were that band who
had a hits with 'Yellow' and 'Trouble'.
ALAN: Coldplay?
HARRY: Freezing, and a very sad ending too.

Which fox puppet is good at cleaning Italian
kitchens after chopping herbs for pesto?
Basil Brush.

CHARITY

I got a letter from my cousin in Africa.
Apparently there's a terrible water shortage out there.
But there's ALWAYS a water shortage out there!
No, but this time it's serious.
How do you know?
The stamp was stuck on with a pin.

He read in the paper that in India it costs just ten pounds to support a child for a year. So he sent his kids there.

He's so mean that when he sends his trousers to the laundry, he puts a sock in each pocket.

CHILDHOOD

We were all great singers in our house.
We had to be.
Why?
There was no lock on the lavatory door.

My parents hated me so much that they got
another kid to play me in our home movies.

One day my parents challenged me to a game of
hide-and-seek. Ten years later I found them in a
town two hundred miles away.

HARRY: When I was a kid, I ran away from home.
It took them six months to find me.
ALAN: Six months? Why?
HARRY: They didn't look.

CHILDREN

BABY 1: I don't think my mum is a very good mother.
BABY 2: Why's that?
BABY 1: 'Cos she keeps getting me up when I'm sleepy, and putting me to bed when I'm wide awake.

Why did the health 'n' safety officer have to measure the baby's biscuit?
He was doing a rusk assessment.

ALAN: Remember that vase you were always worried I might break?
HARRY: What about it?
ALAN: Well, your worries are over.

CHILD: Mum, come quickly! I've knocked the ladder down outside!
MOTHER: Well, don't tell me. Tell your father.
CHILD: I've tried but he can't hear me.
MOTHER: How come?
CHILD: He's hanging from the roof!

CHIP SHOPS

What is the all-seeing deity in the chip shop?
Almighty Cod.

Why is the chip-shop owner like a man with a fancy coat hook?
One has a pickled egg and the other a nickelled peg.

What is the bravest food in the chip shop?
The pickled onion – because it is not a-fried.

Put that fork down and come back and fight like a man!

What is the difference between cheap and crispy chip-shop treats and flying mice with a grudge?
One is batter bits and the other bitter bats.

What did Admiral Nelson say when served the wrong order in the fish shop?
I see no chips.

What do wildebeests use to wrap up their chips?
Gnus paper.

I went into this fish-and-chip shop and I said, 'Fish and chips twice, please!' And the chip-shop owner said, 'I heard you the first time.'

68

Why couldn't the chip-shop owner complete his 'Mississippi' vegetable sculpture?
His Ps were too mushy.

What is the potato's favourite Wild West hero?
Davy Croquette.

CHIP-SHOP OWNER: I've got all my fish lined up ready for opening time.
HARRY: Cod row?
CHIP-SHOP OWNER: Oo, I knew I'd forgotten something.

CHRISTMAS

I thought I said no anchovies!

How does Good King Wenceslas like his pizzas?
Deep and crisp and even.

How do you know if a snowman has been sleeping in your bed?
You wake up wet.

What do angry mice send to each other at Christmas time?
Cross-mouse cards.

Where would you find a reindeer with no legs?
Where you left it.

What does Santa Claus do at Easter?
He egg-nores the whole thing.

I had a terrible row with my wife on Christmas morning. She said, 'You've done absolutely nothing to help with Christmas dinner!'
I said, 'What do you mean? Look at the turkey – I've plucked it and I've stuffed it. And all you've got to do now is kill it and put it in the oven!'

CINEMA

Where does Quasimodo keep his pet rabbits?
In a hutch, back of Notre Dame.

It's not easy being a hunchback but
At least I get a parking place
in the centre of Paris.

Starsky the Rabbit

I've just been pursued by Dr Jekyll's evil alter ego.
Hyde?
You bet I do!

I went to see *Garfield 2* at the cinema but I had
to take my Kia-Ora back – it had a thin layer of
oil and dust floating on it.
Unappealing film?
Well, it wasn't as good as the first one.

What do stuntmen do in their free time?
Just stay home and crash.

CIRCUS

I had a job in the circus, being shot from a cannon. I got 10p a mile plus travelling expenses.

HARRY: My brother's with the circus – he gets £500 a week for swallowing a four-foot sword.
ALAN: What's so good about swallowing a four-foot sword?
HARRY: He's only three feet tall.

I've got this terrific new job in the circus – mucking out the elephants.

Mucking out the elephants! How many of them?

Twenty-five.

Twenty-five elephants! How much do they pay you?

Ten pounds a week.

Ten pounds a week for mucking out twenty-five elephants! If I were you I'd chuck it all in and get a decent office job.

What – and give up show business?

CLOTHES

Why does your top smell of peppermint?
It's a Polo shirt.

Why has your coat got three sleeves?
I bought it from the Arm-y Surplus Shop.

Why couldn't you trust the paper hanky?
It was a tissue of lies.

She's got a dress in her wardrobe so skimpy the moths have to stand on one leg.

Burp!

I told you you shouldn't have eaten that tassle for lunch!

HUSBAND: I hate to say this, but your swimming costume is very tight and very revealing.
WIFE: Wear your own one, then.

COOKING

What are microwaves?
What a flea does when he's saying goodbye.

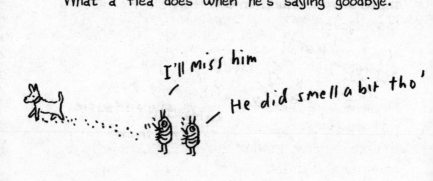

What did the cracked teacup say?
I've been mugged.

My mum makes my soup so thick that when I stir
it, the room goes round.

I said to my mum, 'Where am I when you serve those great meals from which we always have the leftovers?'

I'll never forget the first time Mum made some rock cakes. She passed them round and told me to take my pick. I didn't need a pick, I needed a hammer and chisel.

I've just bought this new juicer and I'm trying it out on everything. Have you ever tried toast juice?

It took me three hours yesterday to stuff a turkey. I was so angry at the end, I could have killed it!

Mmm, my mum's chicken really tickles the palate. She leaves the feathers on.

My mum cooks for fun. If we're hungry we go out to a restaurant!

My mum doesn't need to call us when dinner is ready. We just listen out for the smoke alarm!

My mum feeds me so much fish I've started breathing through my cheeks.

ALAN: I made a rhubarb crumble three feet long.
HARRY: Why so big?
ALAN: I couldn't find any shorter rhubarb!

What do you call someone who's eaten one of my mum's 'specialities'?
An ambulance.

Did you hear about the chef who got an electric shock?
He stood on a bun and a currant shot up his leg.

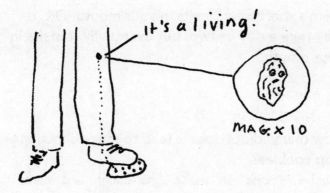

It's a living!

MAG. X 10

MUM: I've got some good news and some bad news. First, I've burned your supper.
HARRY: And what's the bad news?

Any of Mum's leftovers we give straight to the dog. And the dog gives them straight to the cat.

Mum's shortbread melts in your mouth. OK, it may take a day or two, but eventually it melts in your mouth.

How many idiots does it take to make chocolate-chip cookies?
Twelve – one to make the dough and eleven to peel the Smarties.

COWBOYS

What do brainy cowboys listen to?
Rodeo 4.

FIRST COWBOY: Ooh, I feel faint. I've just swallowed a garden snail by mistake.
SECOND COWBOY: Here's a bottle of whiskey – you'd better have a long slug.
FIRST COWBOY: No thanks, the snail was bad enough; I'll have the whiskey though.

CREEPY CRAWLIES

What did the slug Frank Sinatra sing?
'Slimy to the Moon'.

And now as
you carefully fold
your contribution...
... strangers in
the night.

What is the slug's favourite squash?
Slime cordial.

What is the definition of a snail?
A slug with a crash helmet.

can you see what it is yet?

wobble!
wobble!

What did the slug Rolf Harris sing?
'Slimy Kangaroo Down, Sport'.

Which Beatles' song does the snail call home?
'Me-Shell'.

Not a lot of people know that.

What happened when the warty amphibian
parked his car illegally?
It was toad away.

Where do you find giant snails?
At the end of a giant's fingers.

Which hard molluscs have a secret handshake?
Masonry snails.

CRIME

Which fairy-tale character is banned from the Arndale Centre?
Little Red Riding Hoodie.

I've broken European law while wearing strong canvas trousers.
Serious breeches?
That's what I said, didn't I?

JUDGE: I'm sending you to prison for three months.
ALAN: What's the charge?
JUDGE: There's no charge. Everything's free!

What do you call a cheese that is not yours?
Nacho cheese.

JUDGE: For this appalling crime I have no option but to sentence you to twenty-five years in jail.
CRIMINAL: But your honour, I'm sixty-five years old. I'll never live long enough to serve that sentence.
JUDGE: Well, just do the best you can.

HARRY: Our cat's gone missing!
POLICEMAN: Why don't you put a notice up in the park?
HARRY: Don't be silly, our cat can't read!

That's right, I was bluffing... ...I can't read. I merely get the financial Times to impress the neighbours.

A burglar was sent to prison for robbing a bank but he refused to tell the police where he'd hidden the money.

His wife wrote to him in prison and said, 'I need to plant the potatoes, but now you're in prison, there's no one to dig the back garden. I suppose I'll have to do it myself.'

So the robber wrote back to her, saying, 'Don't touch the back garden! That's where I buried the loot!'

A week later he got another letter from his wife. It said, 'You'll never believe it – yesterday thirty policemen came round and dug up the entire back garden!'

And the robber wrote back, 'Now plant the potatoes!'

Two prisoners escaped today. One is seven and a half feet tall, the other four foot three. The police are looking high and low for them.

JUDGE: You're charged with driving at a hundred miles per hour on a motorway.
HARRY: But I wasn't going anything like that speed!
JUDGE: Were you doing sixty?
HARRY: No!
JUDGE: Thirty?
HARRY: No!
JUDGE: Twenty?
HARRY: No!
JUDGE: Okay, I'm fining you £500 for parking on a motorway!

MAN: Can you see a policeman around here?
ALAN: I'm afraid I can't.
MAN: Right then! Stick 'em up!

it's very dark in here!

90

ALAN: Doctor, I can't stop stealing things.
DOCTOR: Take these tablets for two weeks. If that doesn't work, get me a high-definition plasma telly!

Why did the burglar carry a dustpan?
In case he had a brush with the law.

A man escaped from prison by digging a tunnel from his cell to the outside world. When he finally emerged he found himself in the middle of the pre-school playground. 'I'm free, I'm free!' he shouted. 'So what?' said one little girl. 'I'm four!'

Happy Birthday to you!

CROSS TALK

What do you get if you cross a werewolf with a cow?
A burger that bites back.

HA HA
HA HA A Burger that bites back!
HA HA HE HE HO
HO HO!

What do you get if you cross a boomerang with a bottle of perfume?
A smell you can't get rid of.

He crossed a hyena with a parrot so that it could tell him what it was laughing about.

What do you get if you cross a chicken with a guitar?
A hen that makes music when you pluck it.

What do you get when you cross a cow and a duck?
Milk and quackers.

What do you get if you cross a chicken with a dog?
A bird that lays poached eggs.

I OWN THIS TOWN!

What do you get if you cross a cat with a shark?
A town with no dogs in it.

What do you get if you cross a jellyfish with an aircraft?
A jelly-copter.

What do you get if you cross a couple of bananas with a pair of shoes?
Slippers.

What do you get if you cross a skunk and a pair
of rubber boots?
Smelly wellies!

What do you get if you cross a chicken with a
cement mixer?
A brick layer.

Ouch!

What do you get if you cross roast pork with a telephone?
A lot of crackling on the line.

What do you get if you cross a scary creature with a high IQ?
Frank Einstein's monster.

What do you get if you cross a parrot with an elephant?
An animal that tells you everything it remembers.

What do you get if you cross a giraffe with a hedgehog?
An extra-long toothbrush.

I HATE MYSELF!

What do you get if you cross a cat with a dog?
A pet that chases itself.

What do you get if you cross a homing pigeon with a parrot?
A pigeon that asks the way when it gets lost.

What do you get if you cross a carrier pigeon with a woodpecker?
A pigeon that would not only carry messages but also knock on the door when it arrives.

What do you get if you cross a seagull with a
parrot.
A seagull that poops on people on the
beach, but then apologises!

What do you get if you cross a hen with a
parrot?
A hen that lays an egg, then comes over
and tells you about it.

DADS

My dad's so lazy he won't even go outside to see if it's raining. He just calls the dog in and checks if it's wet.

One day a man came to our door and said he was collecting for the children's home. So my dad gave him five of us.

I'll never forget Father's Day last year. I called my dad on the phone, wished him Happy Father's Day and had a really good conversation that went on for ages, all about Mum and when I was a kid and playing in the park and going for rides in the car. It was great.
As we were finally saying goodbye, there was a catch in his voice and he said three words which, as long as I live, I'll never forget: 'Who is this?'

ALAN: Mum, come quick! Dad waded out to sea and now he's up to his ankles in the water!
MUM: That's not very dangerous.
ALAN: It is when he's upside down.

...Blurble-help-
...Blurble!

DANCE

I enjoyed the ballet but I couldn't understand why they all danced on their toes. Shouldn't they just get taller people?

I used to be a tap dancer but I kept falling in the sink.

HARRY: I'm afraid my dancing's not so good. I'm a little stiff from badminton.
WOMAN: I don't care where you're from. Get off my foot!

HARRY: So how did you learn to limbo dance?
MUM: Trying to get into pay toilets free.

DANGER

What's yellow and dangerous?
Shark-infested custard.

What's yellow and sings?
Lark-infested custard.

What's yellow and goes, 'Woof! Woof!'
Bark-infested custard.

What's not yellow but still dangerous?
Shark-infested yoghurt.

What's yellow and grey, smells of bananas and is not dangerous?
A shark eating some banana custard, but don't worry, he won't bite, because banana custard is quite filling.

What's yellow, mushy and smells of bananas?
Shark sick.

DEATH

What is the difference between a musician and a
corpse?
One composes, and the other decomposes.

BABS: My grandad drowned in varnish!
HARRY: What a horrible way to go!
BABS: Yes, but a beautiful finish!

ALAN: I hate you. I can hardly wait till you're
dead so I can dance on your grave!
HARRY: In that case, I want to be buried at sea!

Alan went on holiday, leaving his cat with a neighbour. A few days later he phoned to ask how the cat was doing and the neighbour said, 'The cat fell off the roof and died.'

Alan was very upset and said to his neighbour, 'Couldn't you have broken it to me more gently? The first time I called you could have told me the cat was playing on the roof and fell off and wasn't looking too well, and then broken the bad news to me gradually over a couple of days.'

The neighbour apologised and hung up.

When Alan got home the neighbour rushed out to meet him looking concerned.

'Everything all right?' said Alan.

'How shall I put this, your mother was playing on the roof . . .'

My grandfather's funeral has cost us £12,000 so
far – now I wish we hadn't buried him in a
rented suit.

Why was the cemetery crowded?
'Cos everyone was dying to get in.

 DENTISTS

What is the best time to go to the dentist's?
Tooth-hurty.

Alan's got so many cavities in his teeth, he talks
with an echo.

Mum's got so much bridgework, if you want to
kiss her, you have to pay a toll.

I use striped toothpaste – to make my teeth look longer.

Alan's the only person I know who wears his teeth parted in the middle.

HARRY: So what's the verdict?
DENTIST: Well, your teeth are fine, but your gums have got to come out.

Did you hear about the High Court judge who went to the dentist's?
He asked her to extract the tooth, the whole tooth and nothing but the tooth.

DENTIST: I've got to take a tooth out, but it won't take me a minute.
HARRY: A tooth out? How much will it cost?
DENTIST: One hundred pounds.
HARRY: A hundred pounds? For something that only takes a minute?
DENTIST: Well, I could always take it out slowly.

EXACT CHANGE ONLY PLEASE

The bad news is that my new girlfriend has terrible buck teeth. But the good news is that every time we kiss, she combs my moustache.

Can you recommend anything for yellow teeth? How about a brown tie?

I saw an ad on TV last night for a mouthwash that guarantees to kill all known germs. But who wants a mouthful of dead germs?

DIETS

Mum's idea of a balanced diet is to have a bacon sandwich in each hand.

ALAN: I'll have a banana split made with two bananas, three scoops of vanilla ice cream, chocolate-chip sauce, chopped nuts and big dollop of whipped cream.
HARRY: Would you like a cherry on top?
ALAN: No thanks. I'm on a diet!

He's so fat it takes him two trips to go through a revolving door.

I wouldn't say he was fat, but the other day on the bus he got up and offered his seat to three women.

I'm not saying she's big, but her last picture had to be taken by satellite.

SMILE! MRS

My wife was so fat when we got married that she needed three relatives to give her away. And when I carried her across the threshold, I had to make two trips.

My wife's so thin that when she swallows a Malteser, she looks like she's pregnant.

She's so thin, when she closes one eye, she looks like a needle.

DINOSAURS

If you crossed a Tyrannosaurus Rex, what would you get?
Eaten.

Why are dinosaurs healthier than dragons?
Because dinosaurs don't smoke.

I've stopped smoking and
I'm wearing a patch now

Anti-Smoking patch

What do you call a monster that devours everything in its path?
Lonely.

DIY

How can you swallow a plug?
Gulp backwards.

Why is the concrete lumpy?
Ce-ment to be like that.

Why don't they make nails in China?
Because they'd smash when you tried to
hammer them in.

Why did the drill operator dislike his job?
Because it was bore-ing.

Why are paint tins like fussy mothers on frosty mornings?
They both recommend two coats.

What grows in a pod and can cut through steel?
A laser bean.

What do frogs borrow to do DIY?
Toad's tools.

I don't keep any tools in the van overnight.

Do you know how to make a Venetian blind?
Poke your finger in his eye.

DOCTOR WHO

Where does Doctor Who go to get his salami?
The Dalek-atessan.

Doctor Who's new herbal range was an instant
success. Well, he is a Thyme Lord.

DOCTORS

My doctor (who has nice nails)
just treated a gent from France.
French man he cured?
No, just a clear nail varnish.

ALAN: I can only breathe
through one nostril. I think it's because of
either an allergy to the excellent herbs I
bought or a plug of semi-dried mucus.
DOCTOR: Don't blame it on the good thyme;
blame it on the bogie.

ALAN: Doctor, doctor, I keep thinking I'm a
wigwam and a tepee.
DOCTOR: Calm down, you're two tents!

ALAN: Doctor, doctor, my brother thinks he's a horse. Can you cure him?
DOCTOR: Yes, but it'll cost a lot of money.
ALAN: That's no problem – he's just won the Grand National.

The hypochondriac was complaining to his doctor that he was suffering from a fatal liver disease. 'Impossible,' said the doctor. 'You wouldn't be able to tell. With that disease, there's no pain and you feel perfectly fine.' And the patient said, 'But those are exactly my symptoms!'

HARRY: Doctor, doctor, my hair keeps falling out. Can you give me something to keep it in?
DOCTOR: Certainly, how about this paper bag?

HARRY: Doctor, can I get a second opinion?
DOCTOR: Of course you can. Come back tomorrow.

DOCTOR: Your pulse is as steady as a clock.
HARRY: Maybe that's because you're feeling my wrist watch!

HARRY: Doctor, I get this stabbing pain in my eye every time I have cup of tea.
DOCTOR: Try taking the spoon out.

GRANDAD: Doctor, I'm in great pain from my wooden leg.
DOCTOR: How can a wooden leg cause you pain?
GRANDAD: My wife keeps hitting me over the head with it.

DOCTOR: I can't tell you what's wrong with you. I think it's drink.
ALAN: Okay, I'll come back when you're sober.

The doctor told the patient's wife, 'There's nothing wrong with your husband. It's all in his mind, he just thinks he's ill.'
A few days later the woman phoned the doctor. 'He's got worse,' said the wife. 'Now he thinks he's dead.'

ALAN: Doctor, doctor, it's been one month since my last visit and I still have this itchy rash!
DOCTOR: Did you follow the instructions on the cream I gave you?
ALAN: Yes, it says, 'Keep lid closed tightly closed.'

HARRY: Doctor, doctor, everyone keeps on ignoring me!
DOCTOR: Next, please!

DOCTOR: When you get up in the morning do you have a furry tongue and a pain in the middle of your shoulders and feel terribly depressed?
ALAN: Yes, I do.
DOCTOR: So do I. I wonder what it is?

DOCTOR: You've burnt both your ears! How did it happen?
HARRY: I was ironing when the telephone rang.
DOCTOR: How did you burn both of them?
HARRY: Well, just as soon as I put the phone down, it rang again.

DOCTOR: You've got six months to live.
NAN: But what if I can't pay your bill in that time?
DOCTOR: Then I'll give you another six months.

DOCTOR: Stick your tongue out and say 'Ahhh.'
ALAN: Ahhh!
DOCTOR: Well your tongue looks all right, but why the postage stamp?
ALAN: So that's where I left it!

A woman rang the doctor in a panic. 'Doctor, what can I do? My husband has just swallowed a mouse!'

The doctor said, 'I'll be right over, but while you're waiting, wave a piece of cheese in front of his mouth.'

When the doctor arrived, he discovered the woman waving a fish in front of her husband's mouth.

'I said a piece of cheese, not a mackerel!' he cried.

And the woman said, 'But I had to get the cat out first!'

ALAN: The thing is, doctor, I just feel generally under the weather.
DOCTOR: Maybe it's your diet. What sort of things do you eat?
ALAN: Well, my favourite food is snooker balls. I can't eat enough of them. For breakfast I have a couple of red ones. I have a pink one and a black one mid-morning, then for lunch I have a couple of yellow ones, and for supper some brown balls and some more pink balls.
DOCTOR: Your trouble is you're not getting enough greens.

NAN: Doctor, doctor, I've only got fifty seconds to live!
DOCTOR: I'll be with you in a minute.

HARRY: Doctor, doctor, my son's swallowed a pound coin!
DOCTOR: Why on earth did he do that?
HARRY: I gave it to him and told him it was for his school dinner.

HARRY: Doctor, doctor, I keep on thinking I'm a ten-pound note.
DOCTOR: Try going on holiday – the change will do you good.

HARRY: Doctor, doctor, everybody thinks I'm a liar!
DOCTOR: I don't believe you!

ALAN: Doctor, doctor, you have to help me out!
DOCTOR: Certainly – which way did you come in?

HARRY: Doctor, doctor, everyone says I'm crazy just because I love sausages.
DOCTOR: Of course you're not crazy – I like sausages too.
HARRY: Well, you must come and see my collection – I've got 2,000 of them!

DOCTOR: I have some good news and some bad news.
NAN: What's the bad news?
DOCTOR: The bad news is that you have a horrible new fatal disease.
NAN: Oh no! What's the good news?
DOCTOR: The good news is that we're naming the disease after you and you will become terribly famous.

GRANDAD: Doctor, doctor, I keep on forgetting things.
DOCTOR: When did this start happening?
GRANDAD: When did what start happening?

ALAN: Doctor, doctor, I've just swallowed my mouth organ!
DOCTOR: Thank goodness you weren't playing your piano.

HARRY: Doctor, doctor, can you take my tonsils out?
DOCTOR: Certainly. Would they prefer the zoo or the cinema?

DOCTOR: Stick your tongue out, please.
HARRY: Why? Do you want to examine me?
DOCTOR: No, it's just I've got stamps that need licking.

ALAN: Doctor, doctor, how long can a person live without a brain?
DOCTOR: I don't know – how old are you now?

GRANDAD: Doctor, doctor, my wife thinks I'm a clock.
DOCTOR: Don't worry – she's just winding you up.

HARRY: Here's my new daughter, doctor. You'll have noticed that she has a very long, narrow head and long sticky-out flat ears and a nose that looks like a propeller.
DOCTOR: Plain-looking child?
HARRY: Don't you start!

HARRY: Doctor, doctor, I keep thinking I'm a bridge.
DOCTOR: What's come over you?
HARRY: Two cars, a bus and an articulated lorry.

HARRY: Doctor, doctor, I keep seeing green spots in front of my eyes.
DOCTOR: Have you seen a psychiatrist?
HARRY: No, just green spots.

GRANDAD: Doctor, doctor, I think I'm losing my memory.
DOCTOR: You certainly are – you told me that a couple of jokes ago!

I got my urine tests back. The doctor said they are not normal. I said I suppose going round testing people's urine *is* normal, is it?

ALAN: Doctor, doctor, I keep thinking I'm a cat.
DOCTOR: How long have you thought that?
ALAN: Ever since I was a kitten.

DOCTOR: I want you to stick your tongue out and go to the house next door.
HARRY: Will that help my sore throat?
DOCTOR: No, I just don't like the neighbours.

ALAN: Doctor, doctor, how can I stop my nose from running?
DOCTOR: Simple – hide its trainers!

HARRY: What's up, Alan?
ALAN: I've had bad news. My doctor says I can't play rugby.
HARRY: Really? I didn't even know he'd seen you play! Ha ha!

DOGS

I call my dog Isaiah.
Why?
Because one eye's 'igher than the other.

And the bad news is...
... I need glasses

⊥ Height difference

ISIAH

I took my dog to a flea circus, and he stole the show.

I've been teaching my dog to beg. Last night he came home with 40p.

ALAN: I've got a miniature poodle.
HARRY: A miniature poodle?
ALAN: Yes, the miniature turn your back, he does a poodle.

My dog saw a seat in the park with a sign on it saying WET PAINT. So he did.

My naughty basset hound's just drooled all over an Eastern European leader.
Slobbered on Milosevich?
No, it was Vladimir Putin actually.

HARRY: Hey, your dog's just eaten my hat!
ALAN: Don't worry. He likes hats.
HARRY: I don't like your attitude.
ALAN: It's not my 'at 'e chewed, it's YOUR 'at 'e chewed!

When there's a knock at the door my dog always runs straight for the door – but it's never for him!

ALAN: My dog bit my leg last night.
HARRY: Did you put anything on it?
ALAN: No, he liked it just as it was.

ALAN: My dog plays poker with me.
HARRY: That's fantastic! He must be very intelligent.
ALAN: Not really. Every time he gets a good hand, I can tell because he wags his tail.

HARRY: We've just had our dog put down.
ALAN: Was he mad?
HARRY: He was furious!

In the olden days, before dog leads were invented, you would take your dog for a walk and never see him again. We used to get through thirty or forty dogs a year.

ALAN: My dog chases everyone he sees on a bike. What should I do?
VET: Take his bike away.

Why did the peeping tom steal a pug dog by mistake?
He was trying to take a Peke.

ALAN: I'm going to have a puppy for Christmas!
JEAN: Really? We always have turkey!

Two greyhounds were discussing their skills on the race track. 'I've won eight of my last twenty races,' said the first one.

'That's nothing, I've won thirteen of my last twenty-two,' said the other.

A horse poked its head round the kennel and said, 'Well, I've won ninety-nine of my last hundred races, and I only lost one because I was ill.'

The greyhounds were amazed.

'Wow, did you see that?' they said. 'A horse that can talk!'

Hey I'm in the wrong book!

Tim the Tiny Horse

DOLPHINS

Just how intelligent are dolphins? Well, within just a few weeks of captivity they can train a human being to stand on the side of the pool throwing them fish at least three times a day.

I went swimming with a dolphin but it didn't turn out how I hoped. It got caught in the turnstile.

DRINKS

What do you call very cold water?
Iced water.
What do you call very cold tea?
Iced tea.
What do you call very cold ink?
I know this one . . . Iced ink!
So I've noticed! Have you tried using a
deodorant?

ECOLOGY

The government is finally doing something
about energy conservation. They're asking
motorists to remember to turn off their
windscreen wipers whenever they drive under a
bridge.

I hope you don't mind me asking, but why are
you erecting a barrier round your house?
To prevent flooding.
Noah Fence?
None taken, mate.

Water pollution is getting so bad there's been a
200 per cent increase in the sales of scuba-
diving equipment.
What's so bad about that?
Most of the customers are fish.

ELEPHANTS

What do mammoths wear under their hairy coats?
Ele-pants

Why did the elephant paint himself yellow?
So he could hide in a bowl of custard.
Don't be silly – I've never seen an elephant in a bowl of custard.
See? It works!

Help I'm being eaten by SHARKS!

How do you know when an elephant's hiding in the fridge?
You can't shut the door.

What do you call an elephant
that's small and pink?
A failure!

Sorry, but while you were away an elephant
smashed your best clothes box.
Cedar Trunk?
Of course I saw it, and the tail too – it was
definitely an elephant!

Why did the elephant paint its toenails red?
So it could hide upside down in a bowl of
cherries.

What's grey and wrinkly and goes up and down?
An elephant with hiccups.

What's big, grey and dangerous?
An elephant with a machine gun.

What's grey and has four legs and a trunk?
A mouse going on holiday.

Why do elephants have big ears?
Because Noddy won't pay the ransom.

How does an elephant get down from a tree?
He stands on a leaf and waits until autumn.

Ah. Autumn at last.

Why did the elephant's nose get nicked, driving home from the pub?
Trunk in charge.

How do you get four elephants in a Mini?
Two in the front and two in the back.

How do you get a hippo in a Mini?
Chuck one of the elephants out.

What do you say to a skiing elephant?
Don't say anything. Just get out of the way!

JOHN: I bet I can lift an elephant with three fingers!
ALAN: Prove it!
JOHN: Show me an elephant with three fingers and I'll be glad to.

What's red on the outside, grey on the inside
and very crowded?
A bus full of elephants.

Why is an elephant large, grey and wrinkled?
If he was small, white and smooth, he'd be
an aspirin.

I'm an elephant in disguise

What's the difference between an elephant and
a biscuit?
You can't dunk an elephant in your tea.

EXCUSES
(FOR NOT DOING
YOUR HOMEWORK)

Aliens from outer space took it in order to discover how the human mind works.

HMM... I see 2 times 2 is 4. That explains everything

TABLES

I didn't want to add to your already heavy workload.

My little sister ate it.

I lost my homework fighting a kid who said you were the worst teacher in the school.

Our heating has stopped working, so we had to burn it to keep warm.

EXERCISE

And now for your morning exercises. Ready?
Up, down, up, down, up, down, up, down. And
now the other eyelid.

HARRY: I've got a personal trainer.
ALAN: I've got two – one on each foot.

FAIRIES

Who is the fairy's favourite singer?
Elvish Presley.

ARE YOU GNOME-SOME TONIGHT? ♫

Was the Scottish pixie mean?
No, just eco-gnome-ical.

What do Irish fairies get from wearing pointed pixie boots?
Lepre-corns.

I knew a nymph who went to Calais.
Fairy?
No, Eurostar.

Who runs the Goblins' Hospital?
The National Elf service.

What do Wizards eat for a healthy snack?
Sun-Druid tomatoes.

Why was the fairy's photograph no good?
It was Pixie-lated.

FAMILY

My father used to say, 'Always fight fire with fire', and that's why he was thrown out of the fire brigade.

My family was made up of big eaters – after every meal we had to remember to count the children.

When I was a child I used to rub my parents up completely the wrong way. Because they were made entirely from corduroy.

My mum was a lollipop lady – had a very thin long body and a big round sticky head!

I have a stuffed tiger at home that reminds me of my uncle.
What's it stuffed with?
My uncle.

Little tip for young mums: don't be tempted to take the baby into the bed – there's a chance you might roll onto the baby. And put your back out!

Apparently the cause of ginger hair is if a mother during pregnancy eats too many Cheesy Wotsits.

We were so poor, the tooth fairy used to leave IOUs.

My mum and dad never really got on – my mum was a Time Lord and my dad a Dalek.

I spent most of the day in the garden with my step ladder – not my real ladder, my step ladder.

When I was a kid my family was so poor I had to wear my brother's hand-me-downs – at the same time that he was wearing them.

Don't worry, it'll ride up with wear —

One night my mum tucked my brother up so tightly that when he woke up he was a fossil.

FARMERS

'We're going to have the chicken for dinner,' said the farmer to his family.
'Cool,' said the youngest child. 'Can we teach it to hold a knife and fork?'

YOUNG FARMER: Can you tell me how long cows should be milked?
OLD FARMER: Same way as short cows.

The farmer's new scarecrow is so intimidating that not only have the crows stopped stealing his corn, they're even bringing back the stuff they stole last year.

FASHION

That's an interesting outfit you're wearing. Do you think that style will ever come back?

Seems like Gloria Vanderbilt's daughter has inherited her mother's talent for designing casual trousers.
Denim Genes?
That's the signature line, but she also does lovely seersucker clamdiggers and brocade palazzos.

These one-legged suspender belts are selling well. I repeatedly have to bring more out of the store room.
Keep stocking up?
That's right.

I was so hampered by my unsuitable PE kit that I could feel the warm breath of the second-placed runner on the back of my neck as I crossed the line.
Hot pants right up behind?
Yes – most uncomfortable!

Which cotton reel steals from the rich and gives to the poor?
Bobbin Hood.

FIREFIGHTERS

A fire engine was racing towards an emergency with all its sirens blaring. But as the firefighters looked out of the window they could see a little man jogging along beside them. They turned the engine to full throttle and the sirens to full blast, but no matter how fast they went the little man was still there, running along beside them.

Finally the driver stuck his head out of the window and shouted, 'Why are you following us? What do you want?'

'Two cones, a ninety-nine and a can of cola, please!'

FISH

What do baby sticklebacks play with?
Sticklebricks.

Who was the weakest player in the Greek Fish
Football Team?
Achilles Eel.

What is Peter Stringfellow's favourite fish?
Grey mullet.

Are you taking that lobster home for tea?
No, he's had his tea. Now I'm taking him
to the cinema.

How did the prawn meet his girlfriend?
On the Net.

What was the left-wing Scottish winkle's favourite song?
'Wee Shell Overcome'.

MUM: Why haven't you given the goldfish fresh water?
DAUGHTER: Because they haven't drunk the water I gave them yesterday.

Name two crustaceans.
King's Crus-tacean and Charing Crus-tacean!

Hey, you're not allowed to fish here!
But I'm not fishing. I'm teaching my worm to swim.

A WORM SWIMMING

A WORM SUNBATHING

HARRY: I'm worried there's going to be a flood so I'm building a giant boat to house all my goldfish.
ALAN: Carp Ark?
HARRY: No, a boat.

Why did the oyster write such good poetry?
Because it was Shelley.

FLEAS

Did you hear about the flea who won the
lottery?
He bought a dog in Spain.

How do fleas travel?
By itch-hiking.

LANDLADY: You won't find a single flea in any of my beds.
LODGER: I know. They're all married with families.

What is Grandma Flea's hobby?
Nitting.

HARRY THE FLEA: Shall we walk home?
ALAN THE FLEA: No, let's catch a dog!

FLIES (SEE ALSO RESTAURANTS)

Who takes care of sick mosquitoes?
The Gnat-ional Health Service.

Why was the head-lice's football game abandoned?
The fixture was scratched.

Why do flies buzz?
Because they're always losing their front-door keys.

Why didn't the midge fancy the mosquito?
He was gnat her type.

Have you ever considered double glazing?

FLAT A
FLAT B

No!

Buzz off!

What is the mosquito's favourite hair-product range?
Gnatural Essence.

Why was the Scottish footballer always covered in mosquito bites?
He played in a midge—field position.

It snot funny

FLYING

No matter how bad the in-flight movie, you still shouldn't walk out on it.

The ending was so predictable!

And the characterisations rather thin!

CONTROL TOWER: Please report your height and position.
PILOT: I'm 5 feet 11 and I'm in the cockpit.

This man sitting next to me pointed out of the window and said, 'Look at those people down there. They look like ants.'
And I said, 'They are ants. We haven't taken off yet!'

Last week I flew on one of those new budget airlines. Before we took off, the stewardess reminded us to fasten our Sellotape.

HARRY: I flew to New Zealand!
ALAN: Wow! Didn't that make your arms tired?

FOOD
(SEE ALSO VEGETABLES, CHIP SHOPS)

Why are you carving a tiny boat from fungus?
I fancied mushroom sloop.

Why am I never short of beef fat in my bathroom?
Because the tap is dripping.

What do you call a jelly in a 747?
A jet setter.

Which hero is indecisive when choosing broth?
Soup . . . err . . . man.

What goes 99 thump?
A centipede with a wooden leg?
No, an ice cream being mugged.

Riddle me ree, riddle me ree, why was the old
house encrusted with dried custard?
It had been desserted for years.

What's yellow and stupid?
Thick custard.

How do you start a jelly race?
Say, 'get set'.

Where do they keep the National Pork Dripping
Collection?
The House of Lards.

How do you make a cream puff?
Chase it round the garden.

How do you make a sausage roll?
Push it down a hill.

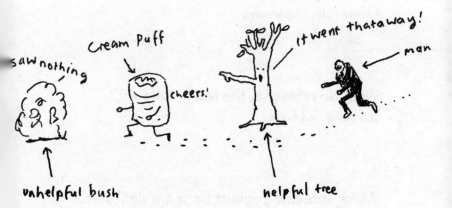

saw nothing

Cream Puff

cheers!

it went thataway!

man

↑
unhelpful bush

↑
helpful tree

What do young Martians pick off their Christmas
cake and discard?
Mars–ipan.

What is 200 feet tall, made of sponge cake,
fruit, custard and whipped cream on top and
stands in the middle of Paris?
The Trifle Tower.

How do you keep food cool in the larder?
Open the sunroof.

What do rabbits at the North Pole eat?
Iceberg lettuce.

Which suckable yoghurt bags are difficult to
undo?
Rubik's Frubes.

Which meat sweetens your breath?
Mince.

Why is there a line of plastic teen dolls waiting
for your Cajun chicken thighs?
It's a Barbie-queue.

Shall I tell you the joke about the butter?
I'd better not – you'll spread it around.

HARRY: I spy with my little eye something
beginning with 'T'.
ALAN: Breakfast.
HARRY: Breakfast doesn't begin with 'T'.
ALAN: You're right . . . sometimes I have orange
juice.

FOOTBALL

What team have never met each other before?
Queen's Park Strangers.

If you have a referee in football, what do you
have in bowls?
Soup.

A football player was walking a cheetah on a
lead. 'Hey, where did you get him from?' a
passer-by asked.
'I won him in a raffle,' said the cheetah.

FROGS

I Just remembered,
I can swim.

How do frogs die?
They Kermit suicide.

What does a frog build a house out of?
Rivets, rivets, rivets.

What's green and goes ninnet ninnet?
A frog with badly fitting false teeth.

What did the frog order at McDonald's?
French flies and a Diet Croak.

Why did the frog say 'Meow'?
He was learning a foreign language.

What's green and goes up and down?
A frog in a lift.

FRUIT

Which fruit does a lot for charity?
Pudsey Pear.

What's yellow on the outside and green on the inside?
A cucumber dressed as a banana.

Bananas are expensive for what they are. After you've skinned them and thrown the bone away, there's nothing left.

ALAN: Has a gooseberry got legs?
HARRY: No.
ALAN: Then I must have swallowed a caterpillar.

What's purple, round and calls out for help in the hedgerow?
A damson in distress.

What happened when someone trod on the grape?
It let out a little whine.

Xmas socks

I have no raisin to be cheerful

Grape

FURNITURE

I've just bought a sideboard made entirely of wool from the unisex barber down the High Street.
Hair Dresser?
No, wool.

ALAN: Is your new settee comfy, Harry?
HARRY (*nodding*): Sofa, so good.

GARDENING

What are you going to do with that horse manure?
I'm going to put it on my rhubarb.
Really? We always have custard on ours!

I know a man who dropped out of tree-surgeon college. He fainted at the sight of sap.

GEOGRAPHY

TONY: So where are you from?
GORDON: Scotland.
TONY: Which part?
GORDON: All of me!

If a person from Poland is a Pole, does that make someone from Holland a Hole?

GHOSTS

How do ghosts begin letters?
Tomb it may concern . . .

What do baby ghosts chew?
Boo-ble gum.

How do ghosts like their eggs?
Terri-fried.

What does a hungry ghost have for tea?
Hunger-arian Ghoulash.

What is the best way for a ghost hunter
to keep fit?
By exorcising regularly.

Did you hear about the stupid ghost?
He climbed OVER walls.

What did one ghost say to the other ghost?
'Do you believe in people?'

When do ghosts usually appear?
Just before someone screams!

Exorcise does you good!

GRANDPARENTS

My nan was supposed to have this oxygen cylinder on at the old folks' home, but because of cutbacks they gave her a snorkel.

Every night my nan calls for French sparkling wine to ease her headache.
Sham pain?
Well I do wonder if she's putting it on a bit sometimes.

My nan was thrown out of the pub for cheating at dominoes. She was found with a pack of bourbon biscuits and bottle of Tippex.

HARRY: My nan's teeth are like the stars.
ALAN: White and sparkling?
HARRY: No, they come out at night.

NAN: Do you like your pocket calculator?
HARRY: Yes, thanks. It will come in useful for
figuring out how many pockets I've got.

My nan gets the telephone mixed up with the
hairdryer. You may have seen her around – wet
hair, chapped lips.

My nan has two left feet, but the up-side is that
she can steal shoes from outside Dolcis.

My nan said, 'Can you help me with this jigsaw?
I can't find the head of the chicken anywhere.'
I said, 'Nan, It's a box of Cornflakes!'

My nan said, 'Who is that little brown man who
sits in the corner of the room and when you
touch his teeth, he sings?'
I said, 'Nan – it's a piano!'

What is the difference between origami and
Grandpa passing wind?
Ones the art of the fold, the other's the
fart of the old.

Grandpa's so forgetful that he went out without
his watch, then looked at it to see if he had time
to go back and get it.

We took Grandad out to the beach at the weekend. It was a bit breezy but we put up one of those cloth screens.

Wind breaker?

I'll say. That's why we mainly do outdoor trips.

GRANDPA: I want to visit my daughter in Australia. How long would it take?
AIRLINE OPERATOR: Just a minute . . .
GRANDPA: That's great news. I'd like a return please!

My nan has got false teeth, so how can I believe a single word she says?

HAIRDRESSERS

My mum's brother just got a well-embarrassing
basin haircut.
Uncool Bob?
That's the fellah.

Mum's got lovely, shiny, long black hair all down
her back. None on her head, just down her back.

ALAN: Aarrgh! Look at the state of my hair!
HAIRDRESSER: But you said you wanted it cut
like David Beckham's.
ALAN: Yes, but David Beckham doesn't have his
hair cut like this!
HAIRDRESSER: He does if he comes here.

HISTORY

What was the mummy's favourite food?
A pyramid of Cheops.

Can I start?

No, wait for your Mummy!

knickerbocker glory for pudding?
Maybe.

Why is it only Tudor buildings that we mock?

Why couldn't the Stone Age man send birthday cards?
Have you ever tried sticking a stamp on a rock?

Which queen burped a lot?
Queen Hic-toria.

Where were the most monarchs crowned?
On the head.

Why did William of Normandy hit the white cliffs
of Dover with a horse chestnut on a string?
He wanted to conker England.

When did King Henry VIII die?
Just before they buried him.

So that's what
his hair looked
like

AAGH!
I'M DYING!

RIP
Hen
VIII

Henry VIII

How can you tell that King Offa was brainy?
He had lots of interesting forts.

Why did Robin Hood steal from the rich?
Because the poor didn't have anything worth stealing.

Why did Hitler only have a flutter on the Grand National?
He thought other races were inferior.

Where were traitors beheaded?
Just above the shoulders.

When King Harold was dying, he put one last arrow in his bow and fired it into the air, telling his men to bury him wherever the arrow landed. So they buried him on top of the wardrobe!

HOLIDAYS

It was a terrible holiday camp. I went to the
office and I said, 'It's about the roof of our
chalet.'
The man said, 'What about it?'
And I said, 'We'd like one.'

The walls were so thin, the neighbours were
dipping their bread in our gravy.

Honolulu – it's got everything: sand for the children, sun for the wife, sharks for the wife's parents.

The resort was so dull, one day the tide went out and never came back.

HOME

I'm not saying the place was messy, but last
week some vandals broke in and tidied up.

Our house was such a mess when I was a kid
that I used to wipe my feet before going out!

The dust was so thick on the floor that the
cockroaches were going round on stilts.

Look at the muck in here!

Last night I dreamed I was eating an enormous marshmallow. When I woke up I'd eaten my pillow.

HARRY: Don't be ridiculous! We can't keep a pig in the house. Think of the smell.
ALAN: Don't worry. He'll soon get used to it.

The house is so old the only thing that keeps it standing is the woodworm holding hands.

What invention allows people to see through walls?
Windows.

HOSPITALS

I had an operation and the surgeon left a
sponge in me.
Did you feel any pain?
No, but I don't half get thirsty!

What did they do before they invented X-ray
machines?
They used to hold the patient up to the
light.

MATRON: Why are you making that patient
jump up and down?
NURSE: Because I've just given him some
medicine and I forgot to shake the bottle!

NAN: So how was it?
SURGEON: I've got some good news and bad news. The bad news is that I'm afraid we amputated the wrong leg.
NAN: Amputated the wrong leg! And the good news?
SURGEON: Your bad leg is getting better.

HOTELS

Which hotel is green, wrinkly and rich in vitamin C?
The Savoy Cabbage Hotel.

Which hotel is salty and brittle?
The Ritz Cracker Hotel.

SNOOTY HOTEL RECEPTIONIST: Do you have reservations?
HARRY: Plenty, but now we're here now and might as well stay.

My room was so small, the mice were hunchbacks. When you put the key in the door, you broke the window!

The walls of our hotel room are so thin you can hear the people next door changing their minds.

HUNTING

HUNTER 1: I say, you've just shot my wife!
HUNTER 2: I'm terribly sorry, old chap. Here, take a shot at mine.

Two hunters come across some lion tracks. One says, 'Follow the tracks to see where he went. I'll go back and see where he came from!'

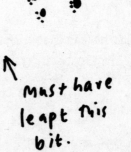

must have leapt this bit.

IDIOTS

ALAN: Why have you got two fried eggs on your head?
HARRY: Because the boiled ones keep rolling off.

An idiot heard that most accidents take place in the home. So he moved.

How does an idiot spell 'farm'?
E-I-E-I-O!

Note on an idiot's door: I'm leaving now. If I
should return during my absence please wait
until I get back.

Did you hear about the idiot Sea Scout?
His tent sank.

You've got your shoes on the wrong feet.
I know. I must have had my legs crossed
when I put them on.

Did you hear about the idiot woodworm?
He was found dead in a brick.

I caught Alan standing in front of the mirror with his eyes closed. He said he was trying to see what he looked like when he was asleep.

I got a local lad to check my rear indicator lights were working. So he stood at the back and I flicked the switch and he said, 'Yes, they are. No, they're not. Yes, they are. No, they're not . . .'

How do you know if you've got an idiot working in the office?
Tippex on the computer screen.

INSECTS

Which TV presenter lives in a labyrinthine underground nest?
Ant.

Do you get this problem with wasps in the supermarket? You're at the checkout and your stuff is going through the scanner but the wasp keeps flying by the scanner and because of its stripey tail it keeps ringing itself up! Beep! Beep! Wasp – 12p.

You know those fine black foam-rubber coverings you get on Walkman earphones? They make an excellent beret for a caterpillar.

INSULTS

You could give an aspirin a headache.

You can brighten up a room – just by leaving it.

You are the excess baggage in the airport
of my life.

You should be on TV – then we could switch
you off.

He's so short, when he pulls his socks up, he can't see where he's going.

He's so short, he's the only man I know who has turn-ups on his underpants.

Small? Let's put it this way: she'd make a great fridge magnet.

He's so tall, he has to stand on a chair to brush his teeth.

The last time I saw legs like those, there was a message tied to them.

With a voice like that, you ought to have your tonsils out.

He's so tall, his brother is a tree.

He's so tall, for six months of the year he goes
around with snow on his head.

not a hairstyle,
a cloud

He's so bow-legged his wife has to iron his underpants on a boomerang.

His wife's bow-legged and he's knock-kneed. When they stand together, they spell the word 'ox'.

He really has an unusual voice. It's like hiccups set to music.

She makes a noise like a cow that just stood on its udder.

He's so ugly Frankenstein's Monster went to a Halloween party as him!

She was so knock-kneed, her legs walked in single file.

INVISIBLE MAN

Did you hear about the invisible man who had children?
He couldn't find them.

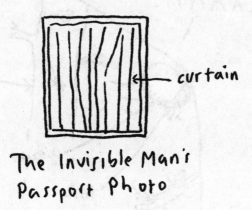

← curtain

The Invisible Man's
Passport Photo

JUNGLE

What's green and hairy and swings through the jungle?
Tarzan of the Grapes.

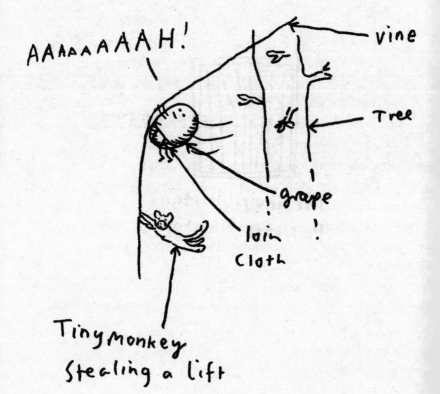

AAAAAAAAH!

vine

Tree

grape

loin
Cloth

Tiny monkey
Stealing a lift

The explorers were making their way through the jungle when they chanced upon a village in a clearing. The villagers rushed towards them with their spears and one of the explorers held up his hand.

'I come in peace!' said the explorer.

'Doo-doo, Dum-dum!' cried the natives.

'Please, I mean no harm to you,' he said.

'Doo-doo, Dum-dum!' cried the natives.

'We come to study your way of life.'

'Doo-doo, Dum-dum!' cried the natives.

'We will film you and make you famous back in our homeland.'

'Doo-doo, Dum-dum!' cried the natives.

Just then the explorer noticed a small herd of elephants at the side of the clearing.

'That's an interesting breed. May I have a closer look at them?'

'Of course,' said one of the natives, 'but be careful you don't step in the doo-doo, Dum-dum!'

On what did Tarzan cross the river?
A gi-raft.

KNOCK KNOCK

Knock, knock.
Who's there?
1 + 1 is Ter.
1 + 1 is Ter who?
Blimey, you're very good at maths for your age.

Knock, knock.
Who's there?
Olive.
Olive who?
Olive in this house, what are you doing here?

Knock, knock.
Who's there?
Wanda.
Wanda who?
Wanda buy a new door bell?

Knock, knock.
Who's there?
Who?
Who who?
Sorry, I don't speak to owls.

Knock, knock.
Who's there?
Roland.
Roland who?
Roland butter's very tasty with a cup of tea.

Knock, knock.
Who's there?
Colleen.
Colleen who?
Colleen yourself up, you're a mess.

Knock, knock.
Who's there?
Romeo.
Romeo who?
Romeover the river, please.

Knock, knock.
Who's there?
Chester.
Chester who?
Chester drawers.

Knock, knock.
Who's there?
Alec.
Alec who?
Alec a nice cup of tea in the morning.

Knock, knock.
Who's there?
Armageddon.
Armageddon who?
Armageddon outta here!

Knock, knock.
Who's there?
Noah.
Noah who?
Noah-counting for taste.

Knock, knock.
Who's there?
Cows go.
Cows go who?
No, cows go moo!

Knock, knock.
Who's there?
Daisy.
Daisy who?
Daisy plays, nights he sleeps.

Knock, knock.
Who's there?
Tish.
Tish who?
Bless you!

Knock, knock.
Who's there?
Heywood.
Heywood who?
Heywood you open the door, I'm freezing!

Knock, knock.
Who's there?
Wenceslas.
Wenceslas who?
Wenceslas bus home?

Knock, knock.
Who's there?
Wayne.
Wayne who?
Wayne a manger, no crib for a bed.

Knock, knock.
Who's there?
Renata.
Renata who?
Renata sugar. Can I borrow some?

Knock, knock.
Who's there?
Bella.
Bella who?
Bella notta working, that's a-why I a-knocked!

Knock, knock.
Who's there?
Alvin.
Alvin who?
Alvin a wonderful time, how about you?

Knock, knock.
Who's there?
Costas.
Costas who?
Costas a fortune to come here, but I'm here
now, so let me in.

Knock, knock.
Who's there?
Falafel.
Falafel who?
Falafel my bike and it really hurt!

Who are you here to see?

Not sure, I just saw the queue and joined it.

An
Aardvark
(I think)

Knock, knock.
Who's there?
Douglas.
Douglas who?
Douglas is broken, can I borrow a cup?

Knock, knock.
Who's there?
Mikey.
Mikey who?
Mikey is stuck in the keyhole!

Knock, knock.
Who's there?
Gorilla.
Gorilla who?
Gorilla me a steak – I'm starving!

Knock, knock.
Who's there?
Amanda.
Amanda who?
Amanda the bed!

Knock, knock.
Who's there?
Cargo.
Cargo who?
No, Cargo vroom, vroom.

Knock, knock.
Who's there?
Annie.
Annie who?
Annie thing you can do I can do better!

Knock, knock.
Who's there?
Norma Lee.
Norma Lee who?
Norma Lee I can let myself in, but I lost my key!

Knock, knock.
Who's there?
Muppet.
Muppet who?
Muppet seven every morning and I still miss the bus.

Knock, knock.
Who's there?
Yvonne.
Yvonne who?
Yvonne you to open the door as soon as possible.

Knock, knock.
Who's there?
Tank.
Tank who?
My pleasure!

Knock, knock.
Who's there?
Astronaut.
Astronaut who?
Astronaut what your country can do for you, but what you can do for your country.

Knock, knock.
Who's there?
Ivor.
Ivor who?
Ivor you let me in or I'll kick the door down.

Knock, knock.
Who's there?
Ivor.
Ivor who?
Ivor ready let you in.
I know – Ivor terrible memory.

Knock, knock.
Who's there?
Irish Stew.
Irish Stew who?
Irish Stew in the name of the law.

Knock, knock.
Who's there?
Jerry.
Jerry who?
Jerry member to leave the key under the mat
like I told you?

Knock, knock.
Who's there?
Cereal.
Cereal who?
Cereal pain having to stand out here like this.

Knock, knock.
Who's there?
Boo.
Boo who?
No need to cry – it's only a 'knock knock' joke.

Knock, knock.
Who's there?
Felix.
Felix who?
Felix my ice cream, I'll tell my mummy!

Knock, knock.
Who's there?
Emma.
Emma who?
Emma new neighbour and I just called round to
introduce myself.

Knock, knock.
Who's there?
Florida.
Florida who?
Florida kitchen is all wet, mind you don't slip
over!

Knock, knock.
Who's there?
Morrissey.
Morrissey who?
Morrissey you, the more I want you.

Knock, knock.
Who's there?
Geezer.
Geezer who?
Geezer kiss.

Knock, knock.
Who's there?
Aardvark.
Aardvark who?
Aardvark a million miles for one of your smiles!

Knock, knock.
Who's there?
Police.
Police who?
Police stop telling these awful knock-knock
jokes!

LETTERS

What did the envelope say to the stamp?
'Stick with me, baby, and we'll go places!'

Stamps are so expensive, I can't afford to write
to my grandma to ask for money!

My postman is very kind: all packages marked
'fragile' are thrown underarm.

LIGHT BULBS

How many psychiatrists does it take to change a
light bulb?
One. But the bulb has really got to want
to change.

How many witches does it take to change
a light bulb?
Just one, but she changes it into a toad.

PATIENT: Every evening, about seven o'clock,
my husband imagines he's a light bulb.
PSYCHIATRIST: Well, why don't you tell him
he isn't?
PATIENT: What, and eat in the dark?!

How many head teachers does it take to change a light bulb?

Two — one to call the caretaker, the other to blame the kids.

How many dentists does it take to change a light bulb?

Two — one to remove the bulb, the other to fill the hole.

How many old people does it take to change a light bulb?

Two — one to change the bulb, the other to tell you how good the old one was.

How many amoebas does it take to change a light bulb?

One . . . no, hang on a minute, two . . . no, four . . . it's eight now . . . sixteen . . . thirty-two . . .

How many Premier League footballers does it take to change a light bulb?

Ask my manager – he arranges all the transfers.

LIKES

Why did the teen like the chewing gum?
Because it was mint.

Why did the raver like elephants?
Because they're large.

When did the psychobilly like her phone?
When it was kickin'.

Why did the toff like the whale's nostril?
Because it was top hole.

LIMERICKS

There was a young man of Calcutta
Who had the most terrible stutter
He said, 'Pass the h-ham
And the j-j-j-jam,
And the b-b-b-b-b-butter'

There was a young lady from Luton
Who purchased a bed called a futon
Each night she retired
Oddly attired
With a shirt and a tie and a suit on

There was a young lady of Tottenham
Who'd no manners, or else she'd forgotten 'em
At tea at the vicar's
She tore off her knickers
Because, she explained, she felt 'ot in 'em

There was an old man from Darjeeling
Who boarded a bus bound for Ealing
He saw on the door,
'Please don't spit on the floor'
So he stood up and spat on the ceiling

There once was a girl called Ruth
Who had her a wobbly tooth
So with a long piece of string
She pulled out the thing
Now the one next to it's loose

A farmer once called his cow Zephyr
She seemed such an amiable heifer
But when he drew near
She bit off his ear
Which made him considerably deafer

There once was a man from Bengal
Who went to a fancy-dress ball
He said he would risk it
And went as a biscuit
But the dog ate him up in the hall

There was a young girl from St Paul
Who attended a newspaper ball
Where her dress caught on fire
And burnt the entire
Front page, sporting section and all

There was a young lady called Hannah
Who slipped on a peeled banana
She wanted to swear
But her mother was there
So she whistled 'The Star Spangled Banner'

MAGIC

How could the Swedish magician's assistant fit into the small steam room?
He'd sauna in half.

Why was the unsuccessful magician hungry at break-time?
He'd forgotten his Twix.

Why did the hip-hop magician say that he hated amusements at Brighton?
He wanted to diss a pier.

MARRIAGE

ALAN: When I grow up, I'm going to marry the girl next door.
HARRY: Lovely! Do you fancy her, then?
ALAN: Not really, but I'm not allowed to cross the road.

LEON: That woman over there must be the ugliest person here.
HARRY: That's my wife.
LEON: Oh dear, I am sorry.
HARRY: *You're* sorry? How do you think *I* feel?

My wife is a stickler for tidiness. I just bought her a cuckoo clock and she's started putting paper under it.

Leona insisted on getting married in her mother's wedding dress. She looked absolutely gorgeous – but her mum was freezing.

PLUMBER: Okay, so where is the drip?
HARRY'S WIFE: He's in the bathroom trying to fix the leak.

Grandpa was reminiscing about his late wife.

'Yes, she was a remarkable woman – extremely religious. When she woke up in the morning she would sing a hymn, then she would say a prayer, then sing another hymn and finish with another prayer. Then, after breakfast, she would say a prayer, sing a hymn, then say a prayer and sing another hymn, and that's how it went on all day – praying, singing and singing and praying. Then, as darkness fell, she'd climb into bed, say her prayers, sing a hymn and say her prayers again. And then, one morning, she was dead.'

'What happened?'

'I strangled her.'

WIFE: Can I have more sleeping tablets for my husband?
DOCTOR: Why?
WIFE: He's woken up.

Every morning I take my wife her tea in my pyjamas. She loves it, but my pyjamas are getting a bit soggy.

- That one please

- yes

This one?

REST IN PEACE

PEACE at LAST

Harry took his friend Steve home for dinner one evening and was greeted at the door by his wife, who flung her arms round him and kissed him passionately.

'That's amazing,' said Steve. 'You've been married all these years and yet your wife still welcomes you home like that.'

'Don't be fooled,' said Harry. 'She only does it to make the dog jealous.'

When people ask me the secret of our long marriage, I tell them. Twice a week we take time off to go this romantic little restaurant we know. There's dinner by candlelight, soft music and dancing under the stars.

She goes on Mondays and I go on Thursdays.

MATHS

A butcher is seven feet tall and wears size 14 shoes. What does he weigh?
Sausages.

What's two-thirds of 99?
The ice-cream man's profit.

TEACHER: If I cut two apples and four pears in ten pieces what will I get?
ALAN: Fruit salad.

MEANNESS

My dad was very mean – he had my mum hypnotised never to order a starter.

Did you hear about the stingy robbers? They did a smash-and-grab raid and would have got away with it but they went back for the brick.

What a party! The wine flowed like glue.

MEDICINE

Why won't you find aspirin in the jungle?
Because of the parrots eat 'em all.

How's your headache?

Better

I couldn't sleep at night so I went to my doctor
and he gave me a strong sleeping tablet. That
night I took two of them and had a really good
night's sleep. When I went into work in the
morning I said to my boss, 'I slept like a log last
night!'
The boss said, 'Great, but where were you
yesterday?'

MONSTERS

What do you call a monster with no neck?
The Lost Neck Monster.

What do you say when King Kong graduates from university?
Kong-gratulations.

What do you do if a monster walks off with your football?
Take up tennis.

What's big and yellow and eats rocks?
A big yellow rock-eater.

What's the best way to stop a stinky swamp
monster from smelling?
Hold its nose.

MOTORBIKES

I've just driven my motorbike down the road
balancing on the back tyre.
Wheelie?
Would I lie to you?

Why don't elephants ride motorbikes?
Their ears won't fit in the helmets.

MOUSTACHES

HARRY: There's a man at the door with a moustache.
MUM: Tell him I've already got one.

Hey, is that a moustache or have your eyebrows just come down for a drink?

When is it okay to spit in a man's face?
When his moustache is on fire.

MUMMIES
(EGYPTIAN)

Why did the mummy go on holiday?
To unwind.

MUMMYS (THE TYPE THAT HANG OUT WITH DADDYS)

ALAN: Mummy, Mummy, why are your hands so soft?
MUM: Shut up and keep scrubbing the dishes!

Mum, do we *always* have to have your metre sticks glued to us?
Yes: while you're living under my roof you'll adhere to my rules.

My mum had one arm a little longer than the other. It did mean she had to wear a slightly built-up mitten.

ALAN: Mummy, Mummy, why are you angry?
I've spent the whole day sitting here reading.
MUM: Yes, but the rest of us would like to use
the toilet too.

ALAN: Mummy, Mummy, I fed the goldfish.
MUM: Yes, but I didn't mean feed him to
the cat.

what's for pudding?
The hamster?

I think I'm
coming down
with
something

MUSIC

What did the orchestra send the conductor
when he was ill?
A get-well-soon chord.

Which composer was good at opening doors?
Handel.

Which opera singer wore a Burberry cap?
Chavarotti.

What's the hungry Chinese headbanger's
favourite sound?
Wok music.

I've just dressed the wounds of the Rolling Stones.
Bandage?
About 357 years if you add them all up.

She's going off to London to have singing lessons.
Where did she get the money?
The neighbours all chipped in.

What do old-skool hip-hoppers put on grazes?
Ghetto plasters.

Why did the composers look under the bed?
They were playing Haydn seek.

What are hippies for?
To keep your leggies up.

I've just been down Hollywood, staying with a
pop star in Ms Monroe's old house.
Marilyn's Mansion?
No, it was that other fellah – you know, Alice
Cooper.

How did the brass band mend their
instruments?
They used a tuba glue.

I've been playing music in the cocktail lounge of
a channel ferry.
P and O?
No, mouth organ.

NAMES

Why have you called your baby Zeus?
He is my 342nd child and it was the only name left in the book.

What do you call a girl who stands astride a river?
Bridget.

BRIDGET!
your dinner's
ready!

I had a brother who was named after my father.
We called him Dad.

What do you call a man with a rabbit
up his jumper?
Warren.

What do you call a man with a shovel
on his head?
Doug.

Doug. meet cliff

What do you call a man without a shovel
on his head?
Dougless.

What do you call a man with a seagull
on his head?
Cliff.

What do you call a man who doesn't sink?
Bob.

What do you call a deer with no eyes?
No-eye deer.

What do you call a deer with one bad eye?
A bad-eye deer.

What do you call a dead deer with no eyes?
Still no-eyed deer.

What do you call a lion with no eyes?
A lon.

What do you call a camel with no hump?
Hump-free.

What do you call a man who's always dipping
biscuits in his tea?
Duncan.

Mummy, Mummy, all the other kids call me a werewolf.
Just ignore them, dear — now wipe your eyes and go and comb your face.

If a fly didn't have any wings, would it be called a walk?

What do you call an Alsatian in a grey jumper?
A plainclothes police dog.

What do you call someone with sausages in their hair?
A headbanger.

What do you call a lady with one leg?
Eileen.

What do you call a girl with a cash register
on her head?
Tilly.

What do you call a boy with a crisp packet
on his head?
Russell.

What do you call a man with a banana
in both ears?
Anything you like – he can't hear you.

NURSERY RHYMES

HARRY: Baa Baa Black Sheep, have you any wool?
SHEEP: What do you think this is? Polyester?

Why did Miss Muffet need a road map?
She lost her whey.

OPTICIANS

Did you hear about the crooked optician?
They sent him to prism.

Why couldn't the shepherdess see her dog?
She was collie-blind.

How do you know carrots are good for your eyes?
Because you never see rabbits wearing glasses!

My eyes are so bad I've got to wear contact lenses just to see my glasses.

My uncle's got a glass eye.
Did he tell you?
No, it just came out in the conversation.

Tell me, have your eyes ever been checked?
No, they've always been blue.

Madonna

I can see your Pants.

Glass eye

Tell me, why do you wear those glasses?
I keep seeing spots before my eyes.
And do the glasses help?
Yes, the spots are much bigger now.

You need glasses!
But I'm already wearing glasses!
In that case, *I* need glasses.

By the way I'M Roger

PETS

ALAN: I'm going to buy a mongoose.
HARRY: Can you get one for me?
ALAN: I would but I don't know the right word
Is it 'mongooses'? Is it 'mongeese'? I don't want
to make a fool of myself.
HARRY: No problem. Just say, 'I'd like a
mongoose, please. And while you're at it, I'll
have another one.'

We called our dog 'Handyman' because he does
odd jobs around the house.

FIRST DOG: What's your name?
SECOND DOG: I'm not sure, but I think it's
'Down, boy'.

ALAN: I used to have a parrot once that laid
square eggs.
HARRY: Did it ever speak?
ALAN: Yes, it said, 'Ouch!'

PIRATES

Where is Captain Hook's treasure chest?
Under his treasure shirt.

Why couldn't the pirate play cards?
Because he was sitting on the deck!

POLICE

What did the policeman say to his stomach?
'Don't move – I've got you under a vest.'

HARRY: Did you see the news? The police are looking for a man with one eye called Roger.
ALAN: What's the other eye called?

POLICEMAN: Blow into this balloon please.
HARRY: Shouldn't that be a bag, officer?
POLICEMAN: Yes, but it's my birthday and I'm having a party.

POLITICS

How does the Conservative Party record their meetings?
They have Da vid Camera on.

He's just the man to get things moving. If he wins, I'm moving.

I hate political jokes – they always get elected.

PRANKS

(You tell your friend:)
Take any number.
Add ten.
Subtract three.
Now close your eyes.
(Your friend closes his eyes.)
Dark, isn't it!

ALAN: What's the difference between an elephant's bum and a postbox?
HARRY: I don't know.
ALAN: Well, I'm not sending you to post any letters.

or That's what I call
PARCEL FORCE!

HARRY: How do you keep a fool in suspense?
ALAN: I don't know.
HARRY: I'll tell you tomorrow.

ALAN: What do brainy people eat for lunch?
HARRY: I don't know.
ALAN: I didn't think you would.

If three pigeons are sitting on a fence and you
shoot and kill one of them, how many will be
left?
Two, of course.
No, there won't. The other two will fly away.

Please add these up:
   One ton of sawdust
   One ton of old newspaper
   Four tons of string
   One half ton of fat
Have you got all that in your head?
Yes.
I thought so.

If you were walking in a field and there weren't
any trees to climb and you didn't have a gun and
you saw a bear heading for you, what would you?
Run.
With a bear behind?

I bet I can jump across the street.
I bet you can't.
(*You walk across the street and jump.*)

Is your house in this street?
Yes.
Better hurry up and move it! There's a car
coming!

HARRY: Ask me if I'm a boat.
ALAN: Are you a boat?
HARRY: Yes. Now ask me if I'm an aeroplane.
ALAN: Are you an aeroplane?
HARRY: No, I just told you I'm a boat.

(As you tell this story, hold one of your hands in front of you, palm up, and trace your journeys with a finger along the lines on your hand as if they were streets. Substitute the street names below for those where you live.)

YOU: I went to the shop to buy a bottle of vinegar and a pound of butter. I walked down the High Street, then over to Harry Street, then down Alan Avenue then Peter Street (*etc.*). When I got to the shop, I bought the butter and the vinegar, and the man put them in a bag, and I started to walk home.

I walked back down Peter Street, up Alan Avenue and then over to Harry Street. Then suddenly I tripped on a skateboard and dropped the bag and broke the bottle of vinegar and the vinegar and butter all mixed together.

Do you know what butter and milk smell like when they are mixed together?

YOUR FRIEND: No.

YOU: Like this! (*You rub your hand in their face – but not too hard!*)

HARRY: Will you remember me in fifty years?
ALAN: Yes.
HARRY: Will you remember me in twenty years?
ALAN: Yes.
HARRY: Will you remember me in ten years?
ALAN: Yes.
HARRY: Will you remember me in five years?
ALAN: Yes.
HARRY: Will you remember me next year?
ALAN: Yes.
HARRY: Will you remember me next month?
ALAN: Yes.
HARRY: Will you remember me next week?
ALAN: Yes.
HARRY: Will you remember me tomorrow?
ALAN: Yes.
HARRY: Will you remember me in another
minute?
ALAN: Yes.
HARRY: Will you remember me in another
second?
ALAN: Yes.
HARRY: Knock, knock.
ALAN: Who's there?
HARRY: You've forgotten me already?

HARRY: Do you know something?
ALAN: No, what?
HARRY: Stupid, aren't you?

Hey, your shirt tail's on fire!
Is it?
(*Pull your friend's shirt out, then say:*) Now it's out!

(*Point to the centre of the palm of one of your
hands. Explain to your friend that the spot you
are pointing to is really a baby and that the
baby is brand new and delicate and needs a lot
of rest. Then say:*)

Daddy says, 'Don't touch the baby!'
Mummy says, 'Don't touch the baby!'
Brother says, 'Don't touch the baby!'
Sister says, 'Don't touch the baby!'

(*and each time point to the spot. Then ask your
friend:*)

'Where is the baby?'

(*When he points to the spot or touches it, shout:*)

'DON'T TOUCH THE BABY!'

ALAN: Bet I can jump higher than a house.
HARRY: Bet you can't.
ALAN: I win. Houses can't jump.

HARRY: Want to see a talking monkey?
ALAN: Yes, please.
HARRY: Take a look in the mirror then.

There was an old man who had a golden arm
because he had lost his real arm in an accident.
And when he died his wife wanted to sell the
arm so she could become rich. So one night she
snuck into the graveyard and dug up the body
and stole the golden arm.

   That night she started having terrible

nightmares and she could hear all these strange noises. The wind was blowing and howling, and then she heard a voice in the distance. And it was like, 'Whooooooo stole my golden arm? Whoooo stole my golden arm? Where is my golden arm?!!'

She locked all the doors and the windows in the house and got into bed and pulled up the blankets up to her head and lay there, scared to death. But the voice kept getting closer and closer, moaning and groaning, 'Whoooo stole my golden arm? Whoooooo stole my golden arm? Where is my golden arm?!!'

And then the door downstairs opened and she heard these footsteps and they got louder and louder and louder. And then the door to her bedroom opened and the footsteps came closer and closer. And she lay there shaking.

Then suddenly she heard the voice again, only now it was right next to her, whispering in her ear. 'Whooooo stole my golden arm?' it moaned. 'Whooooo stole my golden arm? Whoooo? Whooooooo?'

(*At this point pause. Then grab the person next to you and shout:*)

You did!

What is red and goes ding-dong?
A red dingdong.
What is white and goes ding-dong?
A white dingdong.
What is green and goes ding-dong?
A green dingdong.
What is yellow and goes ding-dong?
A yellow dingdong.
No. They don't make them in that colour.

PRISON

My uncle Ronnie is in prison. Last week he had his tonsils out, two weeks ago he had his appendix out and yesterday his wisdom teeth out. He's escaping bit by bit.

LEON: My father went to prison for something he didn't do.
HARRY: What didn't he do?
LEON: He didn't run fast enough.

PRISONER 1: How long are you in for?
PRISONER 2: Seventy years.
PRISONER 1: I'm in for ninety. Since you're getting out first you can have the bed nearest the door.

PSYCHIATRISTS

ALAN: I'm worried. I keep thinking I'm a horse.
PSYCHIATRIST: Well, I think I can treat you. But it's going to cost a lot of money.
ALAN: Money's no object. I've just won the Grand National!

LEON: I just don't seem to be able to get on with anyone.
PSYCHIATRIST: And why do you think that is?
LEON: How should I know, you moron!

MUM: My husband thinks he's a refrigerator.
PSYCHIATRIST: So what's the problem?
MUM: He keeps sleeping with his mouth open and the light keeps me awake.

PSYCHIATRIST: Now tell me, do you normally stir your coffee with your right hand?
HARRY: Oh, yes.
PSYCHIATRIST: Mmm. Most people use a spoon.

HARRY: I keep thinking I'm a packet of biscuits.
PSYCHIATRIST: A packet of biscuits? You mean those little square ones with lots of little holes in them?
HARRY: That's right!
PSYCHIATRIST: You're not mad . . .
HARRY: Thank goodness!
PSYCHIATRIST: You're crackers!

I could murder some cheese

RAILWAY

What's a twack?
Something a twain runs on.

HARRY: Single to Portsmouth, please!
BOOKING CLERK: That'll be nine pounds fifty.
Change at Clapham Junction.
HARRY: I'll have my change here if you don't
mind!

An intercity train was travelling very slowly.
When it stopped suddenly a passenger asked
the conductor, 'Why have we stopped?' The
conductor said, 'There's a tortoise on the track.'
The passenger said, 'But we stopped for a
tortoise ten minutes ago.' The conductor
replied, 'I know – it caught up with us.'

RELIGION

What does God use to smooth off the jagged
edges on the heavenly host?
An angel grinder.

Why does the evangelical papal mission produce
relatively little pollution?
It's got Catholitic converters.

RESTAURANTS

Waiter, what's this fly doing in my soup?
It looks like backstroke, sir.

Waiter, there's a fly in my soup.
Don't worry, the spider in the salad will
soon get it.

Waiter, there's a fly in my soup.
Just wait there, I'll call the RSPCA.

Waiter, there's a fly in my soup.
Yes, it's the heat that kills them.

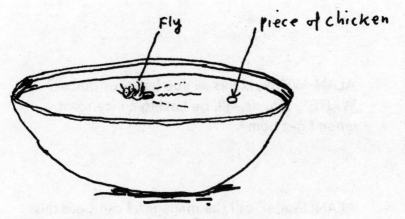

Fly

piece of chicken

Waiter, waiter – there's a fly in my soup!
What do you expect for a pound – smoked salmon?

Waiter, waiter – there's a fly in my soup!
Don't worry, sir – flies have very small appetites.

The truth is I don't even like soup

ALAN: Waiter, is this all you have for dinner?
WAITER: No, sir – I'll be having a nice roast when I get home.

ALAN: Waiter, call the manager. I can't eat this terrible food.
WAITER: There's no point, sir. He won't eat it either.

HARRY: Waiter, there's a twig on my plate.
WAITER: Yes, we have branches everywhere.

HARRY: Waiter, do you serve crabs?
WAITER: Sit down, sir, we serve anyone.

HARRY: Excuse me, will my hamburger be long?
WAITER: No, sir, it'll be round like in the photograph.

WAITER: And how did you find your steak, madam?
DINER: I moved a lettuce leaf and there it was.

Waiter, is there soup on the menu?
No, sir, I wiped it off.

Waiter, this chicken tastes funny.
Why aren't you laughing, then?

... He said 'No you're crackers!'
HA! HA! HA! HA!

HARRY: How dare you belch in front of my wife!
MAN AT NEARBY TABLE: I'm terribly sorry. I
didn't realise it was her turn!

Excuse me, waiter, does the chef have
chicken legs?
No, he always walks like that.

HARRY: There are fingerprints all over this glass!
WAITER: What other part of the body do you
want it washed with?

HARRY: Waiter, what is this?
WAITER: That's bean salad, sir.
HARRY: I know what it's been but what is it
now?

HARRY: Waiter, waiter – this soup tastes disgusting!
WAITER: What are you complaining about? You've only got a bowl of it, we've got a whole pot of the stuff!

ALAN: Waiter, waiter – how long will my chips be?
WAITER: About six centimetres each, I expect, sir.

HARRY: Waiter, have you any wild duck?
WAITER: No, sir, but we have a tame one we could wind up for you.

HARRY: Waiter, I don't like all the flies in this dining room!
WAITER: Well, tell me which ones you don't like and I'll chase them out for you!

HARRY: Wait a minute, what's your thumb doing on my steak?
WAITER: I don't want it to fall on the floor again, sir.

HARRY: I want a sausage burnt on one side to a crisp but uncooked in the middle, some cold baked beans and a fried egg with rock-hard yolk topped with some really gristly bacon.
CAFÉ OWNER: But I can't cook a meal like that!
HARRY: Well, you did yesterday!

HARRY: The service in this restaurant is terrible!
ALAN: Yes, but the food is so bad I don't mind waiting!

What did the frog say when it saw the fly in the soup?
Is that all I get?

HARRY: Waiter, there's a cockroach in my soup.
WAITER: Well, it's the fly's day off.

RHYMES

I'm telling,
You're smelling,
You went to Barbie's wedding.
You kissed her,
You hugged her,
You even said you loved her.
You took her to the sweet shop and bought
    her bubble gum,
And when she wasn't looking
You stuck it up her Ahem! (*Cough*)

Mrs Brown went to town
With her knickers hanging down.
Mrs Green
Saw the scene
And put it in the magazine.

Oooh! Ah!
Lost my bra,
Left it in the vicar's car.

Ha ha, very funny,
My name's Bugs Bunny.

ROADS
(THE CROSSING OF)

What do you call a chicken that crosses the road
to roll in the dirt and then walks back?
A dirty double-crosser.

Why did the fish cross the ocean?
To get to the other tide.

Why did the chicken cross to the middle
of the road?
She wanted to lay it on the line.

Why did the dog cross the road?
Because it was doing an impression of a
chicken.

Why did the turtle cross the road?
To get to the Shell station.

Why did the chicken cross the road?
To get to the other side.

Why did the duck cross the road?
Because it was glued to the chicken.

Why did the hedgehog cross the road?
To see his flat mate.

SO,
HOW you
been?

— a bit flat

Why did the chicken cross the road?
I don't know — it was on the other side
before I got a chance to ask.

Why did the lorry cross the road the wrong way?
It was swerving to avoid the chicken.

Just for the record
I always use a
Pelican

RODENTS

What do dry-skinned gerbils put on their faces?
Mouse-turiser.

Whats the largest mouse in the animal kingdom?
The hippopotamouse.

ROYALTY

Why is the Queen 30 cm tall?
She is a ruler.

ALAN: I'm ashamed to be seen with that Prince
William these days.
HARRY: Ridiculous heir?
ALAN: Yes I really think he should just shave it
off and be done with it.

What does Prince Philip wear on his hernia?
The National Truss.

Why did the Queen buy her husband a new
throne?
To chair him up.

LEONA: I've just married the Queen's son. It was a nice wedding except the groom had an allergy to the salmon, and went all swollen and sweaty.
HARRY: Enlarged glossy prince?
LEONA: Yes, we'll be getting them back from Snappy Snaps any day.

My wife thinks she's the Queen of England.
Have you ever told her she isn't?
What, and blow my chances of a knighthood!

SCHOOL

← Taken shoes off
to help relax

Why is there a hooting noise coming from the
alphabet?
Because of all the v-owls.

LEON: How do you spell chrysanthemum?
HARRY: C-r-i-s-a-n-t-h-i-m-o-o-m.
LEON: That's not how the dictionary spells it.
HARRY: You didn't ask me how the dictionary
spells it.

HARRY: What did you learn in school today?
LEON: Not nearly enough – I've got to go back tomorrow.

LEON: I'm phoning to say I won't be able to come to school today.
TEACHER: Why not?
LEON: I've lost my voice.

HEAD TEACHER: You should have been here at nine o'clock.
LEON: Why, what happened?

Which king had a noisy bottom?
Richard the Lionfart.

LEON: I could be on the school football team if
it weren't for two things.
HARRY: Oh yes, what are they?
LEON: My feet!

TEACHER: Your homework seems to be in your
dad's handwriting.
LEON: Yes, I used his pen.

TEACHER: Leon, I think your dad has been helping you with your homework.
LEON: No, sir – he did it all himself!

TEACHER: What's the most important thing you have learnt in chemistry?
LEON: Never lick the spoon.

Why did the scanner get detention?
For copying.

What's the longest word in the English language?
Smiles — because there is a mile between the first and last letters.

TEACHER: You missed school yesterday, didn't you?
LEON: No, not a bit!

HARRY: Did you have any problems with your French on your school trip to Paris?
LEON: No, but the French certainly did.

TEACHER: Be sure to go straight home.
LEONA: I can't, I live round the corner!

TEACHER: If you were to add 59,725 and 27,640, then multiply by 7, add 12 and divide by 15 what would you get?
LEONA: The wrong answer.

TEACHER: If I had four oranges in one hand and twelve oranges in the other, what would I have?
LEON: Big hands.

TEACHER: Name five animals that live in the jungle.
LEONA: An elephant . . . and four giraffes.

What is black and white and very hard?
An exam paper.

When I was at school why did the teachers get paid when it was the kids who did all the work?

Dad, the teacher shouted at me for something I didn't do!
What was that?
My homework!

Why did the echo get detention?
For answering back.

HEAD TEACHER: Do you know how many teachers work at this school?
LEON: I'd say about half of them.

TEACHER: Don't whistle while you're working.
LEONA: Oh, I'm not working.

What was Shakespeare's favourite part of the school day?
Play time.

Forsooth this is fun!

CALLER: Hello, Headmaster, I'm phoning to say Maxine won't be at school today.
HEADMASTER: Who is this calling?
CALLER: This is my mother.

Why was the school play successful?
It was a class act.

TEACHER: Leon, why are you chewing gum at school?
LEON: To be honest, you're right: I'd rather stay at home and chew it.

What did one maths textbook say to the other?
'Boy, have I got problems!'

TEACHER: If your father earned £2,500 a week and gave your mother half, what would she have?
LEON: A heart attack.

JAMELIA: I'm doing really well at school.
MUM: That's wonderful, darling!
JAMELIA: Yes, today I was first in the lunch
queue!

I really don't like my new school. The teacher
doesn't know a thing – all he does is ask
questions!

Why was the Six Million Dollar Man entitled to a
dedicated teaching assistant at school?
He had special knees.

TEACHER: Now, for homework, I'd like you to write me an essay on Hadrian's Wall.
LEON: Can't I write it on a piece of paper like all the other homework?

HARRY: Does your teacher like you?
LEON: Yes, she keeps putting kisses on my homework.

TEACHER: You, boy, name me two pronouns.
LEON: Who, me?
TEACHER: Correct.

LEON: Please, miss, can I have a glass of water?
TEACHER: No, Leon. That's the fourth one you've asked for in one lesson. Why do you want so many glasses of water anyway?
LEON: I'm trying to stop the fire spreading to the rest of the school.

TEACHER: I hope I didn't see you looking at Leona's exam paper.
LEON: I hope you didn't too!

SCOTS

ANGUS: We took a trip from Scotland to sample the tourist attractions of England's capital.
HARRY: London Eye?
ANGUS: Aye, London, aye.

What is 150 kilometres long, brown, wrinkly and separates England from Scotland?
Hadrian's Walnut.

SEASIDE

What did the harpoonist say when the blubber
went rancid?
Whale oil be off, then.

How is the sea held in place?
Its tide.

What washes up on very small beaches?
Microwaves.

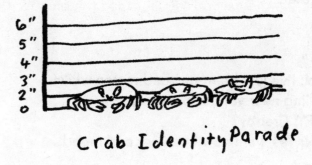

Crab Identity Parade

ALAN: Ow, a crab's just bitten my toe!
HARRY: Which one?
ALAN: I don't know. All crabs look alike to me!

What game is played at the Seaside Wizard
Boarding School?
Squidditch.

ALAN: I've caught a fish for supper.
HARRY: Brill!
ALAN: No, it's a haddock, but good eating nonetheless.

ALAN: I've just been pinched rotten whilst paddling near yonder breakwater.
HARRY: Crabby?
ALAN: Yes, I am now in a very bad mood.

How did the footballing octopus defender save the match?
With his ten-tackles.

How could the harbour master lift up his home?
It was a light house.

How could you tell that the seabird was out of
breath?
It was a puffin.

SHEEP

What do you call a sheep with no legs?
A cloud.

Do you know, it takes three sheep to make a sweater?
I didn't even know they could knit.

Why was the inexpensive lamb happy?
It was sheep and cheerful.

I can't sleep

Try counting Flies.

SHOPS

The inexpensive wastepaper basket I bought
last week has unravelled, but the shop won't
give me my money back.
They say they told me it was a rubbish
bin when I bought it.

MUM: May I try on that dress in the window?
ASSISTANT: Well, we'd prefer it if you used the
changing room.

HARRY: Do you keep stationery?
ASSISTANT: No, I wriggle about a bit.

Did you hear about the man who bought a
paper shop?
It blew away.

HARRY: I want to buy a mousetrap, and could you hurry up because I need to catch a bus.
SALESMAN: I'm sorry, sir, we don't stock them that big.

NAN: Do you have some talcum powder?
CHEMIST: Certainly, madam, walk this way.
NAN: If I could walk that way, I wouldn't need the talcum powder.

Why did the baby fox visit the Arndale Centre after her brush got caught in the door?
For a little re-tail therapy.

GUCCI
TAILS ½ PRICE

I Bet they haven't got a size 16

A big gorilla came into the corner shop and asked for a bar of chocolate.

'That'll be one pound fifty, please,' said the shopkeeper nervously. 'You know, this is the f-first time we've ever had a gorilla in this shop . . .'

To which the gorilla replied, 'I'm not surprised with these prices!'

HARRY: I don't like the look of that monkfish.
FISHMONGER: If its looks you want, buy a goldfish!

A man rushed into the chemist's and said to the assistant, 'Do you have anything that'll stop hiccups?'

The assistant leaned over the counter and slapped the man's face.

The man said, 'What did you do that for?'

The assistant replied, 'Well, sometimes a sudden shock cures hiccups.'

And the man said, 'I don't have hiccups. It's for my wife. She's out in the car.'

SHOW BUSINESS

I've just been beach fishing with the actors from
the panto, but I couldn't get my bait out far
enough to catch any big ones.
Feeble, useless cast?
Well, they're not exactly 'West End'.

Why did the actor put mustard on his ham?
He wanted to try a more challenging roll.

SISTERS

I've got a sister in Australia, so when I phone her
up there's always a slight delay on the line after
I've spoken . . . 'cos she's a bit thick!

When should you put a spider in your
sister's bed?
When you can't find a frog.

My sister thinks I'm too nosy – at least, that's
what she keeps writing in her diary.

My sister told me that you told her that secret I told you not to tell her.

Oh no! I told her not to tell you that I told her!

Well, I told her I wouldn't tell you she told me you told her what I told you not to tell her.

My sister talks so much that when she goes on holiday she has to put suntan lotion on her tongue.

My sister put lipstick on her forehead. She was trying to make up her mind.

I took my sister to the West Indies.
Jamaica?
It's none of your business!

My big sister went on a coconut diet. She hasn't lost any weight, but you should see her climb trees!

SISTER: I'm on a new diet – the pasta diet.
BROTHER: How does it work?
SISTER: Every time I get hungry I walk right pasta the fridge.

LEONA: I'm on an even newer diet – the seafood diet.
ALAN: How does it work?
LEONA: When I see food, I eat it.

SPACE TRAVEL

What powers your mum's
sister's space craft?
Auntie-matter.
How did she get it?
She won it in the NASA
summer fair tombola.
What is it called?
The STARSHIP AUNTY-PRIZE.

What does the astronaut
have for breakfast?
An unidentified frying
object.

What is an astronaut's favourite TV show?
COUNTDOWN.

If an astronaut spits his chewing gum out of the window of his spaceship, what do you call it?
A chew F O!

What do you do if you see a spaceman?
Park in it, man!

What kind of poetry do astronauts write when they are in space?
Uni-verses.

Did you know that scientists are planning a visit to the sun?
Yes, to prevent themselves being burnt they will go at night-time.

What is an astronaut's favourite game?
Moon-opoly.

How does the astronomer cut his hair?
E-clipse it.

What did one shooting star say to the other?
'Pleased to meteor!'

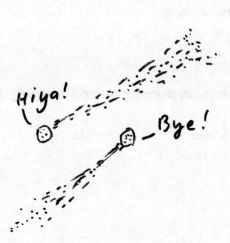

Hiya!

Bye!

Why was the thirsty astronaut hanging around the computer?
He was looking for the space bar.

What are the best days to visit space?
Sundays and Moondays.

What's the quickest way to speak to someone on Saturn?
Give them a ring.

What's the most popular name for a pub on Mars?
The Mars Bar.

What did the astronaut say when he saw the
fleet of spaceships coming?
'Here come the spaceships!!!'

How do astronauts get their baby to fall asleep?
They rocket.

How do solar systems hold up their trousers?
With an asteroid belt.

SPORT

ALAN: What time shall we meet at the leisure centre?
HARRY: Tennish?
ALAN: Actually I fancy a swim.

Ah, there's been some confusion....

What goes white and red, white and red?
An England rugby player rolling down a hill.

How did the washing powder get out at cricket?
Bold.

How did the Old Bailey judge get out at cricket?
Court.

How did the water in the leaky bucket get out
at cricket?
Run out.

Why did the amateur pool player have loads of
change in the turn-ups of his trousers?
He kept missing the pockets.

A cricket walked into a sports shop.
'Hello,' said the sales assistant. 'Do you know there's a sport named after you?'
'You mean there's a game called Alan?' said the cricket.

Why did the roller-dude force a flat fish to listen to the cricket on the radio?
He wanted to make a skate-board.

SUPERMAN

Why does Superman hate new technology?
Have you ever tried to change into a blue
suit and cape behind a mobile phone?

SWIMMING

I thought I could trust the people who use my pool, but all I know is that when I filled it last year I put in 10,000 gallons and when I emptied it last week I took out 11,000 gallons.

HARRY: I'm going swimming after my lunch.
ALAN: Really? I'm getting mine from the canteen.

TELEVISION

HARRY: I do like *Coronation Street* and the
actress who played Bet Lynch. What's her real
name – Julie . . .? Julie . . .?
ALAN: Goodyear!
HARRY: Not bad, but I'm looking forward to
Christmas.

When I was a kid we didn't have a television, so
my dad bored a hole through the wall into the
house next door and we used to watch the
wrestling every night – till we discovered that
the neighbours didn't have a television either.

I did my first television show a year ago and the very next day one million television sets were sold. And the people who couldn't sell theirs threw them away.

I watched a very thought-provoking programme on television last night. The thought it provoked was, 'Why am I watching this programme?'

Which TV presenter lies around on the boat all day?
Dec.

TIME

Why does a candelabra sound like a clock?
Because the candles tick.

A crazy-looking guy asked me the time. 'Eight
fifteen,' I said.
'I think I'm going nuts,' he said. 'All day
long I've been getting different answers.'

TRAVEL

HARRY: I'd like a return ticket, please.
BOOKING CLERK: Certainly, sir. Where to?
HARRY: Back here of course!

I waited ages for a number 36 bus. But it never came.
So what did you do?
Well, eventually two number 18s came along, so I got on them.

What is the difference between the Scottish pixie taxi company and an unsuccessful bodybuilder?
One's got wee cabs. The other weak abs.

It was a very windy day in the Himalayas and a Sherpa spotted a young mountaineer floating down under a parachute. 'That's very dangerous,' he told the mountaineer. 'Coming down here in a parachute.'
'But I didn't come down in a parachute,' protested the mountaineer, 'I went up in a tent!'

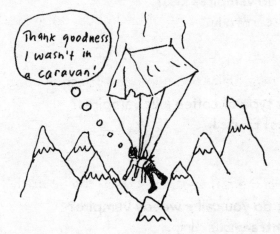

I'm visiting a family of beavers in a lake in Holland.
Hamster dam?
No, Maastricht.

VAMPIRES

What does Dracula's torch run on?
Bat-teries.

How do vampires kiss?
Very carefully.

What type of coffee kills vampires?
De-coffinated.

What do you call a weedy vampire?
An intravenous drip.

Who is Dracula most likely to fall in love with?
The girl necks door.

How does Dracula help a baseball team?
By turning into a bat.

What is Dracula's favourite milkshake flavour?
Vein-illa.

VEGETABLES

What is the flag of the British Shallot Society?
The Onion Jack.

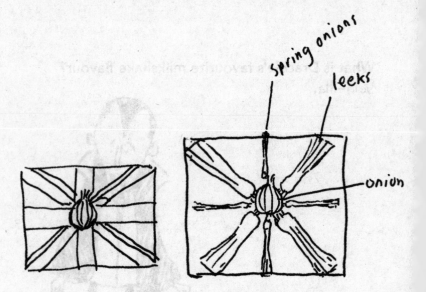

spring onions

leeks

onion

You coming to Ascot this year?

Why do you think I'm wearing this ridiculous hat?

Why were the peas so wealthy?
They were minted.

Why did the tomato blush?
Because it saw the salad dressing.

I Didn't know where to look!

ALAN: I don't like cabbage and I'm glad I don't like it.
HARRY: Why's that?
ALAN: Because if I did like it, I'd eat it – and I hate the stuff!

Who looks after the labour interests of the shallots?
The trade onions.

What do you call two parallel lines of vegetables?
A dual cabbageway.

Did you hear about the rebellious wheat plant?
It got its ear pierced.

My lodger is a vegetable.
You mean . . .?
Yes – he's a herbaceous boarder.

FIRST HARICOT: How are you?
SECOND HARICOT: I've bean better.

Bean 1

you've looking a little BROAD

Bean 2

Yes I need to go for a run.

VETS

What did the vet squeeze out of the cuttlefish's boil?
Octo pus.

How did the vet know it was okay to use the dead octopus's organs for transplant?
It carried a squid-ney donor card.

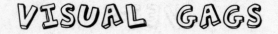

VISUAL GAGS

What am I?

(Move your right pointing finger around and around your right ear. With each turn, stick more and more of your left pointing finger into your mouth.)

I don't know.
A pencil sharpener!

What's this?

(Snapping your fingers, move both hands wildly around your head.)

Beats me.
Two butterflies with hiccups.

WEATHER

It was so cold last night that I fell out of my bed
and cracked my pyjamas.

You know it's below freezing when you comb
your hair outside and it breaks!

Did you have any trouble in the floods?
I'll say. I had to float out of the bedroom
on my double bass.
And what about your wife?
She accompanied me on the piano.

It was so windy the other day, one of our hens laid the same egg six times.

It was so cold the hens were laying eggs from a standing position.

WHAT IS THE DIFFERENCE?

What is the difference between a model automobile and a shy sailor?
One is a toy car, the other a coy tar.

What is the difference between a fruit-and-nut chocolate bar and a man with a shed up his nose?
One is a hazel nut, the other a nasal hut.

What is the difference between a shepherd's evening delight and a pasty made from fat-tailed lizards?
One is a pink sky, the other a skink pie.

What is the difference between school 'roast'
and a genetically modified research apiary?
One's got peas like bullets, the other's got
bees like pullets.

What is the difference between a bamboo
model of Nelson's Column and a paracetamol?
One is a cane pillar, the other's a pain
killer.

What's the difference between a dirty young
fellow and pasteurised Chinese bean sauce?
One is a soiled boy, the other boiled soy.

Bits of Tripe

THe 'TRIPEY' smile

What is the difference between your grin with bits of your dinner stuck between your teeth after eating the stomach lining of a cow, and a zebra crossing 1.6 km (approx) wide?
One's a tripey smile, the other a stripey mile.

What's the difference between a vegetarian treat and a coconut-shy proprietor with tired feet from standing up all the time?
One is a coleslaw sarnie – the other a sole-sore carny.

What is the difference between those cardboard
trays that purple squashy fruits are packed in
and the larger sizes of vixens?
One is fig boxes, the other is big foxes.

What is the difference between a lord of the
manor with purple hair and sunglasses and a
chip-shop owner with a high-pitched voice?
One is a freaky squire – the other a
squeaky fryer.

What is the difference between the Cardiff Millennium Centre and Bambi?
One is a Welsh idea, the other a well-shy deer.

What's the difference between an unknown Christmas benefactor and a big ray with no sense of fun?
One is a mysterious Santa, the other's a serious manta.

What is the difference between illegal bare-knuckle boxing bouts and the number of evenings Jesus spent in the wilderness?
One is naughty fights, the other is forty nights.

WITCHES

What do you call a witch who lives by the beach?
A sand-witch.

Why do witches fly on broomsticks?
Because their vacuum cleaners don't have long-enough cords.

How does a witch tell the time?
She looks at her witch watch.

Why did the angry witch land with a bump?
'Cos she lost her temper and flew off the handle.

What's evil and ugly and goes up and down
all day?
A witch who accidentally picked up a pogo
stick instead of a broom.

What happens when you see twin witches?
You find it difficult to tell which witch is
which.

What do witches say when they overtake each other?
Broom, broom, broom!

What subject do witches enjoy at school?
Spelling.

How do witches keep their hair in place?
With scare spray.

What did the witch ask for when she booked into the hotel?
A broom with a view.

ZOMBIES

Why did the zombie get arrested for eating muesli?
They thought he was a cereal killer.

What do zombies like on their chops?
Grave-y.

What do Italian zombies eat?
Maggotty Bolognaise.

What did one zombie say to the other?
'Get a life!'

AGGGH! COCO POPS! I hate you! You turn the milk Brown!

Zombie-type

Run!

crushed corn flake packet

loose corn flakes

piece of toast who thinks it is a broader vendetta.

AND EVEN MORE JOKES!

H. HILL
BESPOKE JOKES TO THE GENTRY
BY APPOINTMENT TO HER MAJESTY THE PEARLY QUEEN ELIZABETH OF HACKNEY
ALSO I ONCE MET THE CHUCKLE BROTHERS
HILL TOWERS
LONDON

Dear Readers,

Thanks for sending in all your jokes. As promised, here are some of my favourites.

Remember, when you're laughing at these jokes, it's important to try and imagine the person who sent it in. You might like to draw a picture of what you think they look like, then travel to the place where the jokester lives and see if you can spot them.

Alternatively, you might just decide to do something more interesting instead.

Thanks for all the laughs,

Harry Hill

READER'S JOKES

How do you get a redhead's attention?
A ginger snap.

Emily Paxby, age 15

What do you get when you cross a lemon with a deer?
Sourdoe.

Emily Molli, age 15

Why does Gail from *Coronation Street* always point her finger?
Because she is E.T. and wants to phone home.

Hannah Copson, age 12

Five little pigs go out to dinner one night. They look at the menu and the waiter comes to take their order:

PIG 1: Two orange juices, two lemonades and lots of water for him.
WAITER: Then what?
PIG 1: Ermmm, a pizza to share, except for the pig who is drinking all the water.

The waiter brings the food and asks the pigs what they want for dessert.

PIG 1: We will have ice cream, but he will still have just water.
WAITER: Why does he just want water?
PIG 1: Well, one of us has to go wee wee wee wee all the way home!!

James, Birtley Book Crew, Birtley Library

What do you get if King Kong steps on Batman and Robin?
Flatman and Ribbon.

Harry Wilson

What's a rabbit's favourite dance style?
Hip Hop.

Bethany, Birtley Chatterbooks group

Why did the monkey fall out of the tree?
It was dead!

Why did the second monkey fall out of the tree?
Because it was hit by the first one!

Why did the elephant fall off her skateboard?
BECAUSE SHE WAS HIT BY FALLING MONKEYS!!

Meghan, Birtley Chatterbooks group

Why did the lizard go on a diet?
It was too fat for the scales.

Daniel, Birtley Chatterbooks group

What do you call a sweater hanging from the top of a mountain?
A bungee jumper.

Alexander, Birtley Chatterbooks group

What sort of music do bankers listen to?
Northern Rock.

Jonathan, age 11

Do you want to hear a story about a blunt pencil?
Nahh . . . it's pointless.

Ashley Price, age 9

Once there was a magic slide, and whatever you said when you went down it appeared at the bottom. One man said 'Gold!' and he landed in a pot of gold. The next man said 'Beer!' and he landed in a pint of beer. However, the last man didn't know it was a magic slide so he said 'WHEEEE!!!' and he landed in the toilet.

James Gautrey

A short-sighted old lady was looking for the Electricity Board showroom. By mistake she wandered into the local pet shop and approached the manager.

'I'd like an infra-red griller,' she said. The manager looked at her in puzzlement for a minute.

'I'm afraid we haven't got one of those,' he said, 'but I can let you have a nice ultra-violet chimpanzee.'

Amethyst, age 11

What did the fake fish say to the marlin?
I know someone who could help you out with that big nose. My brother is a plastic sturgeon.

David Lyall

What do you get if you mix a sheep with a Dalek?
A Baalek.

Alfie Case-Thompson, age 5

What did the skeleton say to the toilet?
You can't get nothing out of me!

Jayden Neil-White, age 10

What's red and sits in the corner?
A naughty strawberry!

Patrick Sproull

A man is sitting in a bar enjoying a relaxing evening when his hand starts vibrating. The man starts talking into his palm and the barman looks round.

'What are you doing?' he asks curiously. The man doesn't answer but continues talking to his hand whilst more people look round. After a little while the man puts down his hand and the barman asks again what he was doing.

'I have recently been on a trip to China,' explains the man, 'and when I was there, I had a chip installed in my hand which works the same way as a mobile phone. I can call anywhere in the world with my palm and I get 250 free texts a month with O2!'

The barman says it's all lies and that the man is just a sad loser who craves attention, but the man says he'll prove it. He asks for the bar's telephone number and starts tapping different parts of his palm, then lifts his hand to his ear. The bar's phone rings and it's him, crystal clear. The barman goes off to tell some other people about this amazing hand whilst the man nips off to the loo. Ten minutes pass and the man is still not out of the toilet so the barman gets a little worried. When it reaches the 15-minute mark, the barman sends a regular to the lav to see what's happening. When the local walks in, he is surprised to see the man standing against the wall with a toilet roll up his bum. He asks him what he is doing and the man says, 'I'm waiting for a fax to come through!'

Joe McNeice, age 13

What do you call a Cuban with a tummy upset?
Castro Enteritis!

Juliette

I used to be a werewolf but I'm alright nowooOOOOOO!

Molly Walker, age 8

Harry goes to the barber's, and sees a poster with a picture of the barber's beautiful hair. It says, 'BALDIES! FOR JUST £50, I CAN MAKE YOU LOOK JUST LIKE ME!' Harry goes inside and pays the barber to do what it says on the poster. Then, the barber sits down and shaves off all his hair!

Bradley, age 12

Why don't skeletons play music in church?
Because they've got no organs.

Robert Yates

What do you call a blind dinosaur?
A Doyouthinkhesawus!

Sam Clarke, age 10 and Charlotte Edwards, Wales

An Englishman, an Irishman, a Scotsman and a German all went on a plane. The Englishman dropped a brick out of the window, the Irishman dropped a stone, the Scotsman dropped a knife and the German dropped a bomb.

The Englishman got home and found his dad crying in the garden.

'Dad! What's the matter?' he asked.

'Your mother and I were out gardening, when a brick fell from the sky and hit her on the head. Now she's dead!' said the father.

The Irishman got home and also found his father crying in the garden.

'Dad! What's the matter?'

'Your mum and I were out gardening. A stone fell from the sky and hit her on the head. Now she's dead!'

The Scotsman got home and found his dad crying in the garden.

'Dad! What's the matter?' he exclaimed.

'Your mother and I were out gardening when a knife flew from the sky and hit her on the head. Now she's dead!'

The German got home and found his dad laughing hysterically in the garden.

'Dad! What's so funny?' the German asked his father.

'Well,' said the father. 'I was out gardening, when I farted and next door's house blew up!'

Jessica James-Eyers, age 11

What's the difference between Brussels sprouts and bogies?
You can't get kids to eat Brussels sprouts.

Freya, age 16

Why was Tigger looking down the toilet?
He was looking for Pooh!

Amber Kirk, age 11

Why couldn't the chicken cross the road?
Because some idiot left his chewing gum on the pavement and it got stuck to his little chicken feet and, sadly, he got run over!

Jenny Louise Pearce

DONALD: My canary died of flu.
DORA: I didn't know birds could die of flu.
DONALD: Mine flew into a car.

What happened to the man who put his false teeth in backwards?
He ate himself.

Why don't ghosts make good magicians?
You can see right through their tricks.

What does a toad use for making furniture?
A toad's stool.

Rhys, age 11

Three frogs go into a hotel. They ask the receptionist if there are any rooms. There aren't any rooms, so they go to sleep inside a bathroom instead. One frog sleeps in the toilet, one in the bath, the other in the sink. When morning comes, the frog in the sink asks the frog in the toilet, 'What was it like down there?'

The frog in the toilet replies, 'Well, first it went dark, then it rained, and then a log fell on me.'

Zara Rowden, age 13

Why is Cinderella no good at football?
Because her coach is a pumpkin!

Estelle Warner, age 7

Why did the one-handed man want to cross the road?
To get to the second-hand shop.

Samuel Wade

Knock, knock.
Who's there?
Interrupting cow.
Interrupting co . . . MOOOO!!!!!!!!

Isabel Collins

Why did the banana go to the doctor?
Because he wasn't peeling very well.

Louis, age 5

A man bought a very expensive talking pet
centipede for company. Once he got it home he
said to the centipede, 'Let's go to the pub for a
pint.'
    The centipede didn't respond so the man said a
little louder, 'Let's go to the pub for a pint.'
    Still no response from the centipede, so he
shouted, 'I said, let's go to the pub for a pint.'
    The centipede replied, 'All right! I heard you the
first time. I'm getting my shoes on.'

Jamahl Franklin, age 11

Knock, knock.
Who's there?
Nobody.
Nobody who?
.... (silence)
HeHeHeHe

What is Thomas the Tank Engine's favourite railway station?
Tooting.

Ophthalmology Explained by I. C. Clearly

Toilet Training for Beginners by P. P. Pants

Sunday Breakfasts by Roland Bacon

Nutritional Lunches by Roland Soup

Who Done It by F.U.N.E. Clues

Get Rich Quick by Rob Da Bank

Niamh Roberts, age 9

What did the water say to the boat?
Nothing, it just waved.

Lucy Morrison, age 9

What did the policeman say to his tummy?
You're under a vest!

Jenny-Mai Fletcher Chan, age 8

Why did the child study in the aeroplane?
He wanted a higher education.

What's red and flies and wobbles at the same time?
A jellycopter!

Ryan Gauld, age 8

What is a mummy's favourite type of music?
Wrap music.

Jane Thomas

What machine allows you to eat and listen to music at the same time?
The pie pod.

Luke Morris, age 10

What did the taxi load into its DS?
A car-tridge.

Charlie Hills, age 7

What is the most common illness in Yogurt Land?
Petit Flu.

Edward Hills, age 9

What did the frog have for breakfast?
French flies and Diet Croak.

Campbell Gillespie

What do you get hanging from apple trees?
Sore arms!!!   HA HA HA

Why did the chicken cross the road?
Because he wanted to get to the other
side!!! HA HA HA

What do you get if you pour hot water in a rabbit
hole?
Hot cross bunnies!!!   HA HA HA

Why did the zebra cross the road?
Because there was a zebra crossing!!!!   HA
HA HA

Ella Hunter, age 6

Moses, Jesus, and an old man were playing golf. Moses went first. He teed up, swung, but the ball landed in a water trap. He cursed, then parted the water and went in to retrieve the ball. Next went Jesus. He teed up, swung, and like Moses, the ball landed in the water trap. He didn't curse, but thought. Then he walked across the water, and retrieved his ball. The old man came last. He teed up, swung, and like Jesus and Moses, hit the ball into the water trap. But then a fish swam over and ate the ball. A hawk swooped down and ate the fish, and just as it was flying away, the hawk got struck by lightning. It disintegrated, and only the ball was left behind. The ball fell and landed in the hole. Jesus turned to the man and said, 'Nice shot, Dad!'

Francesca Bertoletti, age 11

CONGRATULATIONS!!! You have just won the weight of your brain in sweets!
To claim your Tic Tac, go to www.sweetsforever.com

Theo Lewthwaite, age 12

HARRY: I nearly chopped my finger off making dinner last night – I didn't even turn a hair!!
ALAN: I'm not surprised – you're bald.

Charlotte Sonkur, age 13

There are two monkeys in an airing cupboard.
Which monkey is in the army?
The one on the tank.

Leah Blackwell, age 8

Why do bees have sticky hair?
Because they have honeycombs!

Helen Gore, age 8

A plane crashes on the Mexican border. Where do they bury the survivors?
You don't bury survivors.

Andrew Duncan

There were three tomatoes, Mummy tomato, Daddy tomato and Baby tomato. They went on a walk. Daddy and Mummy were far ahead and Baby tomato was lagging behind so Daddy ran to Baby tomato, squished him, then said 'Ketchup, baby!!!'

Bethany Dawn Booth, age 11

What did Batman say to the Evil Chef?
I'm going to put a stop to your villainous flans!!

James Michael, age 9

What do you say if you get into trouble for not doing your homework?
You can't tell me off for something I didn't do!

Kay Hamersley, age 13

ACKNOWLEDGEMENTS

Most of these jokes have been with us for longer than any of us can remember so thanks to all the joke writers living and dead who have unwittingly contributed to this book.

Thanks to Peter Quinnell, who has written some great new jokes.

To my researchers Winnie and Kitty Hall for combing the joke books for me.

To Magda too for pointing me in the right direction in so many things.

To Janet Staplehurst for her secretarial skills.

To Stephen Page, Julia Wells, Donna Payne and all at Faber, and to my copy-editor Trevor Horwood for some helpful contributions.

Have you enjoyed *Harry Hill's Whopping Great Joke Book*?

Want something even sillier?

Then put on your running shoes and rush out and buy:

HARRY HILL'S BUMPER BOOK OF BLOOPERS

DEAR MILKMAN,
BABY ARRIVED YESTERDAY,
PLEASE LEAVE ANOTHER ONE

P.G. Police Say Detective Shot Man With Knife

Washington Post

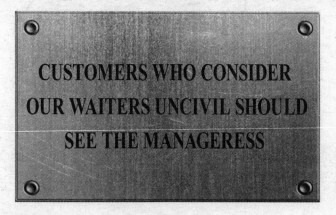

Sign in restaurant

A comic caper that every 9-11 year old aspiring comedia
will love packed with comedy dos and don'ts!